Listening and Learning

Listening and Learning

Practical Activities for Developing Listening Skills   Grades K-3

Bernice M. Chappel

Fearon Teacher Aids
a division of
PITMAN LEARNING, INC.
Belmont, California

ISBN-0-8224-4306-6

Printed in the United States of America.

1.9 8 7 6 5 4 3 2 1

Table of Contents

Foreword

Listening is the most important factor in a child's acquisition of academic skills, in learning how to communicate effectively, and in gaining the ability to relate to others in a mutually satisfying manner.

Proper listening habits begin in the home, almost from birth. Yet too many children enter kindergarten as poor listeners, with poor communication skills and with little ability to relate appropriately either to peers or to adults. Teachers become frustrated by their inability to reach many of these children. Too often these children seem uninterested, refusing to take any active part in the learning of needed academic and social skills.

Why is it that the task of motivating learning in children seems more difficult now than in the past? Many of the reasons may be related to the tense, almost overstimulating pace of modern life.

Nowadays, children are extremely dependent upon stimulating visual approaches to learning. Television exposes them to a constant parade of visual and auditory excitement. Magazines filled with photographs and beautifully illustrated children's books present them with opportunities for firsthand viewing of interesting activities and ways of life. These and other factors combine to give a child an insatiable appetite for ever more exciting visual experiences.

As a result, many children come to school markedly underdeveloped in some of the most basic human qualities. They come unable to listen to their inner thoughts, by which they can perceive and share their feelings as well as those of others. They come unable to pay attention unless a stimulating visual approach is present. They come untrained in the capacity to follow directions.

First, we must accept children as they are. But through a planned program, we can gradually teach new attitudes that will enhance the learning of academic skills.

One of the first steps is to teach *ourselves* to be good listeners. Our facial expressions will show just how interested and attentive we are when talking and listening to a child.

We must also let children know that we place a high value on good listening habits. This may be done easily by making frequent comments such as "I really enjoyed reading that story to the class today. Everyone seemed so interested," or "Mark, you're certainly a good listener. I always enjoy answering your questions."

We also need to repeatedly emphasize courtesy in listening. Children need to learn that it is impolite to interrupt a speaker or to fail to listen when someone is addressing them.

Young children need help in preparing for listening. Distracting toys or other objects should be put away before an activity or story is started. Children should be made aware that they're expected to remain seated during brief stories and discussions. In order to reinforce standards, the goals and reasons for listening should be frequently discussed with the group. Children should be reminded that it is just as important to listen to themselves and each other as it is to listen to the teacher.

Listening and Learning has been prepared as an aid to busy teachers of primary-age children, teachers who recognize the need for intensive training in listening skills. It is designed for use in brief periods, varying from five to fifteen minutes, with each lesson complete in itself.

The illustrations in this book are meant to be used only by the teacher. The children are to be encouraged to visualize and to use their imaginations—to listen carefully for "word pictures." These experiences improve concentration, creative thinking, and verbal skills, and they reinforce training in recall and the expression of original thoughts. These outcomes provide the teacher with insights into the child's values and attitudes. They are few paper-and-pencil tasks in this book. The games, activities, stories, poems, and rhymes are designed primarily to improve the listening and oral skills.

Listening and Learning, planned to entice children into desirable listening habits, is divided into three sections. Section I contains activities and games; Section II has original poems and rhymes; Section III consists of stories and storytelling exercises. The exercises in each section are arranged in the order of difficulty, starting with Kindergarten and progressing through Grade 3.

You will find the "Correlate with" suggestions helpful in reinforcing a concept. As an example, Exercise 13, "Bus Station," is planned to teach skill in listening and in following directions. At the end of the activity you are referred to two other lessons that are directed to the same objectives, namely, Exercise 18, "Follow My Directions," and Exercise 70, "Emergency." The sequential numbers that identify the exercises make it easy to find correlated activities.

The questions and discussion topics at the end of the poems and stories in Sections II and III are intended as a guide to stimulate the children's thinking. You may choose to use one or all of them. You may also use your own approach to achieve the objectives of the exercise.

If you keep the acquisition of learning skills in mind in your daily work with your children, desirable benefits are sure to follow. Group discussions will help the children develop an awareness of the feelings of others, proper listening etiquette, original and creative thoughts, the ability to relate, the capacity to contribute to group solutions to common problems, and qualities of leadership. In addition, individual children will profit from the sharing of knowledge.

When you help your children to learn to listen, you give them a powerful tool that they will use in academic and social situations. You give them the gift of listening to learn more about a rapidly changing and fascinating world.

Bernice M. Chappel
Brighton, Michigan

You will find the correlations to be helpful in reenforcing a concept. As an example, Exercise 13, "Bus Station," is planned to teach skill in listening and in following directions. At the end of the activity you are referred to two other lessons which also are directed to the same objectives, namely, Exercise 18, "Follow My Directions," and Exercise 70, "Emergency." The sequential numbers which identify all exercises are for the purpose of making it easy to find correlated activities.

The questions and discussion topics at the end of the poems and stories in Sections II and III are intended only as a guide to stimulate the children's thinking. You may choose to use one or all of them; or, depending upon the make-up of your group, you may use an entirely different approach to reach the objectives of the exercise.

If you will keep the acquisition of listening skills in mind in your daily work with your children, desirable benefits are certain to follow. Group discussions will develop an awareness of the feelings of others, proper listening etiquette, original and creative thoughts, the ability to relate, the capacity to contribute to group solutions of common problems, and the flowering of qualities of leadership. In addition, the individual child will certainly enhance his store of information.

When you help children to gain good listening skills, you give your pupils a useful and necessary tool for every aspect of social and academic existence. The ability to be a good listener results in more productive and satisfying living for one's entire lifetime.

Bernice M. Chappel
Brighton, Michigan

What Makes That Sound?

Dd Ee Ff Gg Hh Ii Jj K

How Many Claps?

SECTION 1

Activities and Games

1. What Is It? (K-1)

Listening Experience: Using verbal clues

Collect a number of familiar objects such as pencils, crayons, erasers, marbles, buttons, beads, bottle caps, keys, chalk.

Have seven or nine children participate at one time. Three players sit in a circle while a helper stands behind each player with a blindfold. After the helpers have blindfolded their players, a leader is chosen. He puts an object into the hands of each player and makes a simple clue statement about the object. About a crayon or pencil he might say, "We use this to make pictures."

The players try to identify the objects. When all of the objects are identified, the helpers who were standing take their turns as players and each retiring player chooses a new helper. A new leader is chosen. The round is completed and new rounds follow as long as time permits and interest continues.

2. How Did I Get to School? (K-1)

Listening Experience: Using nonverbal clues

Say to the children: "There are many ways to get from one place to another. Let's think of ways we might get to school. As you think of ways, show us how you would get here. We will watch and listen carefully."

Children may demonstrate walking fast, walking slowly, skipping, jumping, or other methods.

After a discussion of the ways demonstrated, the children put their heads down on their desks. A child is chosen "to go to school." After he crosses the room he calls, "How did I get to school?"

The children guess. One of those who guessed correctly is chosen to go to school, and the game continues.

3. What Makes That Sound? (K-1)

Listening Experiences: Listening intently. Identifying familiar sounds.

Say to the children: "Sometimes we don't hear sound because we are thinking of something else. Put your head down and listen carefully. Try to think what I am doing to make each sound. Raise your hand when you think you know what I'm doing."

Among things you might do to produce familiar sounds are the following:

Opening a window Writing on the chalkboard
Dropping a book Cutting cardboard with scissors
Bouncing a ball Pouring water into a container
Dropping a pencil Flipping the pages of a book
Sliding a chair Closing a window softly
Crumpling paper Dropping coins on a desk
Shuffling your feet Opening a desk drawer

4. How Many Claps? (K-1)

Listening Experiences: Listening while counting. Hearing and remembering.

The children close their eyes while a leader claps his hands a number of times. The children listen and count silently. The leader calls on individuals and asks, "How many times did I clap?" If the child answers correctly he becomes the next leader.

Variation:
■ The leader may clap in a pattern, like: "Clap, pause, clap, clap." The expected answer then is, "One clap and then two claps. One clap and two claps make three claps."

5. Where Are the Owlets? (K-2)

Listening Experiences: Recognizing voices. Perceiving direction and distance of sound.

Three children are selected by the leaders to be Wise Old Owls. They leave the room. Five children are chosen to be owlets—they will do the talking. All children put their hands over their mouths, so that it can't be seen who is talking and who is not.

The leader calls the Wise Old Owls to return. They say, "Who? Who? Who?" The owlets reply, "Who? Who?"

The owls listen, then tap a child they think replied. If they are correct, the tapped child removes his hands from his mouth and the owls continue searching for the remaining owlets by saying, "Who? Who?" until all five owlets are located.

The Wise Old Owls select three children to take their places and the game continues.

Correlate with: Lesson 42, "The Owl."

6. What's Going On? (K-2)

Listening Experiences: Perceiving sounds in the immediate area and paying attention to them. Becoming aware of routine sounds and talking about them.

Say to the children: "There are sounds about us all the time, but sometimes we don't think about them. Let's put our heads down and close our eyes. We'll be very quiet and listen. We'll try to hear every sound and remember what we've heard. At the end of two minutes we will raise our heads and tell what we've heard."

After the children have raised their heads, ask, "What sounds did you hear?"

Children may give such answers as coughing, traffic, music in the next classroom, shuffling feet, a train whistle, a bus horn, the wind, children in the hall, water running in the lavatory.

Variation:

■ This activity may also be used outdoors. It is especially effective for a rest period during a nature hike.

7. Cats and Kittens (K-2)

Listening Experiences: Recognizing disguised voices. Perceiving direction of sounds.

The leader chooses seven children to be cats. The remainder of the class are kittens.

The cats stand at the front of the room with their backs to the kittens. The leader points to a kitten, who disguises his voice as he says, "Mew! Mew!"

If a cat thinks he knows the identity of the kitten who mewed, he raises his hand. The leader calls him by name, as, for instance, "Arnold Cat." The cat has three guesses. If he wishes the kitten to mew again the cat says "Meow!" If the cat guesses correctly, he sits down and the kitten becomes a cat.

The game continues as long as time permits or as interest is maintained.

Correlate with: Lesson 16, "Stealing the Cat's Mouse"
Lesson 12, "Detectives"
Lesson 69, "The Rescue"

8. Who's Coming to the Party? (K-2)

Listening Experience: Distinguishing different voice qualities by attentive listening.

Begin by choosing a child to be the party-giver. The party-giver sits at the front of the room and must keep his back to the class. The leader then quietly chooses a child to be the guest, who then goes behind the party-giver and knocks on his chair.

The party-giver inquires, "Who is it?"

The guest replies, "Good morning, [John]. I'm coming to your party."

If the party-giver can name the guest, he continues. If he fails to identify the guest's voice after two attempts, the guest becomes the party-giver.

If the children enjoy playing this game they can make it harder by disguising their voices.

9.   Which Animal? (K-2)

Listening Experience: Paying careful attention in order to use several items of information to make a judgment.

Say to the children: "I am thinking of an animal. Listen carefully until I am finished. Then tell me what animal I am thinking of.

"This animal is very large. It has a gray hide with no fur. It has large floppy ears and a short tail. It is strange-looking— it seems to have a tail at both ends. What animal am I thinking of?" (elephant)

The first child who replies correctly when called on becomes the leader and presents a description of an animal of his choice.

Variations:

■ Describe buildings, trees, or other objects instead of animals.

■ Describe people.

10.   Hello, Mrs. (Mr.) Ear (K-2)

Listening Experience: Distinguishing different voice qualities by attentive listening.

This game is enjoyed by all children of elementary school age.

A child is chosen to be Mrs. (or Mr.) Ear. She stands with her back to the class. The leader points to someone to start the game. The selected child addresses Mrs. Ear with two short sentences, one of which gives a guarded clue to his identity, as, "Hello, Mrs. Ear. I have brown hair."

Mrs. Ear has three chances to identify the speaker. If she is successful she may have another turn. If she is not able to identify the speaker, Mrs. Ear sits down and the speaker becomes the next Mrs. (Mr.) Ear.

11. Pass It On (K-3)

Listening Experiences: Receiving a whispered message.
Recalling a message correctly and repeating it accurately.

Begin by whispering a sentence to a child, who whispers it to another, and so on to the last child, who then tells the class what he heard. Then you tell the class what your original sentence was.

The game continues with individual children starting original sentences.

Kindergarten and first grade should usually have short sentences, but second and third grades may be successful with longer sentences. Mature groups may be able to repeat two or three short sentences accurately.

This activity is most interesting if sentences are constructed so that they tell interesting news about a classmate, as, "John has a new baby sister," or "Nancy is going to the circus tomorrow."

Variation:

■ The teacher or a child whispers a sentence about a familiar story.

12. Detectives (K-3)

Listening Experience: Locating a hummed sound from
a distance.

The teacher or a leader chooses three detectives, who leave the room while the class selects someone who will hum. Everyone, including the hummer, covers his mouth with his hands.

The detectives are summoned and the hummer starts to hum a tune. The detectives try to locate the hummer, who may stop humming if the detectives come too near him.

If a detective is successful in locating the hummer, he becomes a player, the hummer becomes a detective, and the game continues.

13. Bus Station (K-3)

Listening Experience: Hearing, understanding, and
responding to directions involving
"right" and "left."

Choose someone to be "it." Any number of players sit on chairs in a circle. The child who is "it" stands in the center of the circle and calls, "Everyone right!" or "Everyone left!"

The players get up and move in the direction called, while "it" tries to get a vacant seat. His opportunity comes when a player starts in the wrong direction.

When "it" succeeds in getting a seat, the unseated player is the next "it." He moves to the center of the circle and the game continues.

Correlate with: Lesson 18, "Follow My Directions"
Lesson 70, "Emergency"

Bus Station

Flying

14. Say Something Nice about Someone (K-3)

Listening Experience: Hearing an example and producing a comparable verbalization.

This activity is a valuable way to spend a few minutes while waiting for a bell to ring. Depending upon the social adjustment of the group, it may be used as often as you need.

Start the discussion with the explanation that recently you have seen and heard several people in the room doing or saying something helpful or kind. For example, "I saw Jack help a child on the playground who had fallen and hurt his knee," or, "Sally picked Ann's coat up from the floor and Ann said, 'Thank you.'"

Children are asked to volunteer incidents of polite or helpful acts or remarks which they have recently observed.

After two or three brief sessions of this type, children will be more aware of polite, helpful behavior and of the pleasure it brings to all participants.

Correlate with: Lesson 30, "Guess Who"
Lesson 66, "The New Coat"
Lesson 67, "The New School"

15. Flying (K-3)

Listening Experience: Hearing and discriminating between possible and impossible statements.

The children stand beside their desks. The leader stands at the front of the room. As he moves his arms rapidly up and down like wings he may say, "The airplane is flying."

The children move their arms up and down each time the leader makes a statement about something which flies (jets, helicopters, kites, or various kinds of birds or insects).

If the leader names something unable to fly, the children must not move their arms in the flying motion under penalty of sitting down until the next leader takes over. After about ten directions are given, the leader may choose someone to take his place.

Variations:

■ Discuss flying animals such as bats, flying fish, flying foxes and flying squirrels. For variety, occasionally include them in the original game.

■ Play the game using only birds as the flying objects.

16. *Stealing the Cat's Mouse (K-3)*

Listening Experience: Perceiving faint nonverbal sounds.

A child chosen to be the cat sits at the front of the room with his back to the class. Under the cat's chair is a mouse. (An eraser makes a good mouse.) The cat must try to prevent his mouse from being stolen, but he must not turn around.

The leader signals to a player to begin. The player sneaks up behind the cat. If the cat hears the thief coming, he mews, "Meow!" The player returns to his seat without the mouse. If the cat mews when there is no thief, another cat takes his place.

If the thief succeeds in stealing the mouse, the cat turns, faces the class, and tries to guess who stole his mouse. He gets three guesses. If he guesses who the thief was, he continues being the cat. If he fails to identify the thief, the successful thief becomes the next cat and the unsuccessful cat becomes a player.

Correlate with: Lesson 7, "Cats and Kittens"
Lesson 69, "The Rescue"

17.   A Halloween Game (K-3)

Listening Experiences: Recognizing disguised voices.
Locating the source of a sound by
direction and volume.

A child is chosen to be a witch (or warlock). The witch leaves the room while a leader chooses three children to be ghosts and three to be black cats. All the children cover their mouths so that it cannot be seen who is talking and who is not.

After the leader summons her, the witch says, "Where are my ghosts and black cats?"

The ghosts must say, "Boo, Boo!" in a scary voice. The cats must reply, "Meow, Meow!"

The witch circulates about the room, listening intently as she frequently asks, "Where are my ghosts and black cats?" When she thinks she has identified a ghost or cat, she taps him. If she is correct, the child stands up.

When all the ghosts and cats have been identified, the witch selects someone to take her place and the game continues.

Variations:

- "A Christmas Game." Santa and helpers. Santa says "Ho! Ho! Ho!" and the helpers must reply "Merry Christmas!"
- "An Easter Game." Easter Bunny and helpers. Bunny says "Where are the Easter eggs?" and helpers must reply "Here! Here!"

Correlate with: Lesson 5, "Where Are the Owlets?"
Lesson 7, "Cats and Kittens"
Lesson 44, "The Steam Goblin"
Lesson 47, "A Haunted House"

18. Follow My Directions (K-3)

Listening Experience: Hearing, remembering, and
executing a series of directions.

Begin by giving a series of two or more directions for a selected child to execute. If a child successfully completes the directions, he (she) chooses the next player. All the directions in any series are given at the same time and should not be repeated.

The difficulty of the activity should be determined by the maturity of the group. In some groups, two simple directions may be sufficient. Other classes may be able to carry out a longer series of directions, such as: "Walk ten steps to your right, go to the blackboard, draw a circle, then skip to your seat."

With most third-grade groups, directions may be given involving north, south, east, and west, as well as right and left. Other commands may involve doing an arithmetic problem on the chalkboard, spelling a word, or performing some task about the room.

In kindergarten, first grade, and second grade, the teacher may give the directions. Third-grade children should be able to handle this exercise without teacher assistance.

Correlate with: Lesson 13, "Bus Station"
Lesson 70, "Emergency"

19. At the Supermarket (K-3)

Listening Experience: Hearing, remembering, and
expanding a sequence of
statements.

The children pretend they are shopping at the supermarket. The first child says, "I went to the supermarket. I put a loaf of bread (or any item the child chooses) in the cart."

The second child continues by repeating the item named by the first shopper and adding another, as, "I put a loaf of bread and a dozen eggs in the cart." The third child repeats the purchases of the first two shoppers and adds her item.

If a child can't recall the items or the correct order, she may choose a volunteer to take her turn.

With kindergarten children, three items may be the maximum number they can handle at one time. Numerous shopping trips may be started until each child has had an opportunity to participate.

Variations:

- "Leaving the Supermarket." "At the checkout counter, I took the bread out of the cart," and so on until the cart is empty.
- "Toy Chest." "I took the building blocks out of my toy chest," and so on.
- "Going for a Walk." "I went for a walk and I saw a fire engine," and so on.

20. Health Rules (K-3)

Listening Experience: Hearing and obeying directions.

The children stand beside their chairs. The game leader (or the teacher) gives directions involving a good health practice. The leader, using his own name, gives a command like "Bobby says, 'Wash your hands before eating.'" Then Bobby and the other children make the motion of washing their hands. Further commands might be, "Bobby says, 'Brush your teeth,'" and so on through any number of health rules. The children follow only the directions preceded by "Bobby says." If the leader omits these words, those who perform the motion must sit down. When most of the children are seated, another game may be started with a new leader and all the children again taking part.

Possible commands include: take a bath, go to sleep, eat fresh vegetables, eat _____ (specifying some food), drink a glass of milk, wash your face, touch your toes, and so on.

21. Remembering Names (K-3)

Listening Experience: Hearing names of classmates.

In the first days of a new school year the class may be divided into two rows facing one another. Point to a child in one row, and ask the first child in the opposite to tell the given name of the child. If the child does not know, another child is asked and the child who missed gets another chance later. Follow the same procedure with the first person in the other row. The activity proceeds until all children have had a chance to call out a name.

When the children have mastered the given names of class-mates, repeat the game with surnames.

22. Look and Remember (K-3)

Listening Experience: Hearing and seeing a sequence of items and repeating it.

Remembering Names

Mickey Mole
and
Ollie Earthworm

Arrange from three to five objects (the number depends upon the ability of the group) before the children. The objects may be classroom supplies such as a book, a pencil, crayon box, chalkboard eraser. Tell the children to watch and listen as you point to and name the objects from left to right. They now name in unison the objects before them as the teacher points to them. (Always proceed from left to right.) Next, ask the class to study the order in which the objects are placed and to try to remember it.

After approximately one minute, remove the objects, and have the children attempt to recall the order in which the objects were arranged.

The first child to name the sequence correctly becomes the next leader and takes the teacher's place. He arranges the objects in a different order and the game continues.

23. *Mickey Mole and Ollie Earthworm (K-3)*

Listening Experience: Perceiving direction of sounds.

The children form a circle and choose one child to be Mickey Mole and another to be Ollie Earthworm. Both children are blindfolded and placed in the center of the circle.

Mickey Mole tries to catch Ollie Earthworm. He (she) calls, "Ollie, where are you?"

Ollie Earthworm must reply, "I'm right here, Mickey."

Both children depend entirely upon hearing to determine the location of the other — Mickey in trying to catch Ollie and Ollie in trying to elude Mickey.

When Mickey catches Ollie, both children choose replacements for themselves and the game continues.

Correlate with: Lesson 60, "Mickey Mole"

24. I'm Thinking (1-2)

Listening Experience: Recognizing beginning sounds in words and recalling words with same beginnings.

Say to the children: "I'm thinking of the name of something in this room. It's a word that starts with the same sound that *baby* starts with. Can you guess what it is?"

Children might guess, "Is it a *boy*?" You might reply, "No, it is not a *boy*." The children continue guessing, using words that start with the sound of *b*, until someone says, "Is it a *book*?" The teacher says, "Yes, it's a *book*."

The child who thought of the correct word becomes the leader and the game continues.

Correlate with: Lesson 31, "Ear Sharpeners"

25. Riddles (1-2)

Listening Experiences: Paying attention to a group of clues. Finding words from rhyme clues.

Explain to the children that riddles are something like puzzles, in that clues (pieces) properly put together create a mental picture which gives the answer to the riddle.

The riddles may be used in any order. It is unlikely that you will wish to use the entire exercise at one time.

Children will enjoy reviewing old riddles before you go on to the follow-up questions.

I am very tall. I am green in summer. Birds nest in me. I give shade when the sun is too hot. Sometimes I become part of a house or a fence or a chair. I rhyme with *three*. I'm a _____. (tree)

I am a building. Horses live in me. I rhyme with *table*. I'm a _____. (stable)

I live in a pond. When I was very young I was a tadpole. I rhyme with *log*. I'm a _____. (frog)

I am a small animal. I am gray. I say, "Squeak! Squeak!" I rhyme with *house*. I'm a _____. (mouse)

I am an animal. I have a bushy tail. I climb trees and eat nuts. I rhyme with *girl*. I'm a _____. (squirrel)

I am an animal. I have a bushy tail. I hunt birds and small animals. I am smart. I look a little like a dog. I rhyme with *box*. I'm a _____. (fox)

I am red, white, and blue. I have thirteen stripes. I have fifty stars. I rhyme with *bag*. I'm the American _____. (flag)

I'm big and orange-yellow. I'm very hot. I'm in the sky. I rhyme with *fun*. I'm the _____. (sun)

I am a bird. I hunt at night. I eat mice and insects. I rhyme with *howl*. I'm an _____. (owl)

I am round and rocky. Sometimes I look yellow, and sometimes I look silver-white. You usually see me at night. I recently had some visitors from your country. They left me a flag. I rhyme with *balloon*. I'm the _____. (moon)

Oral Questions and Discussion:
This follow-up activity uses the answers to the riddles — *tree,*

stable, etc., to answer the first question, and other clues in the riddles to answer the second question—*birds, horses,* etc.

- What rhymes with *three?* What nests in a tree?
- What rhymes with *table?* What lives in the stable?
- What rhymes with *log?* What do we call a frog when he is very young?
- What rhymes with *house?* What color is a mouse?
- What rhymes with *girl?* What does the squirrel eat?
- What rhymes with *box?* Tell something about a fox.
- What rhymes with *bag?* How many stars are in the flag?
- What rhymes with *fun?* What color is the sun?
- What rhymes with *howl?* Tell something about an owl.
- What rhymes with *balloon?* How is a balloon like the moon?

Correlate with: Lesson 38, "Making Riddles"

26. The Seasons (1-2)

Listening Experience: Understanding statements and recognizing them as true or false.

Print YES and NO in large letters on the chalkboard. After you read each statement below, a designated child points to *yes* if the sentence is true and to *no* if it is not true. The child who replies should be asked to explain his thinking. Some answers will vary depending on geography, each child's experience, customs, etc.

We see snow in winter.
Leaves fall from the trees in spring.
Birds build nests in the spring.
Children have a long vacation from school in summer.

Christmas comes in the fall.
The Fourth of July is celebrated in the summer.
Birds fly south in the spring.
Children rake leaves in the summer.
People work in their gardens in the winter.
People swim in the lake in the winter.
Apples and peaches are ready to be picked in the spring.
Easter comes in the fall.
Halloween comes in the fall.
Valentine's Day comes in the winter.
New Year's Day comes in the fall.

27. Shopping (1-3)

Listening Experience: Listening to a speech sound and recognizing it when it is heard again.

After children have had instruction in phonics, the teacher can introduce listening activities which emphasize recognizing specific sounds as they appear in pronounced words. Since this is strictly an oral-aural activity, children are not required to spell the words, but rather to identify the sounds. The teacher accepts matching sounds regardless of their spelling— *salt* and *cereal* for /s/, *sugar* and *shrimps* for /sh/, *tea* and *beef* for /ē/. It is best to work only with sounds in accented syllables.

The teacher says, "We'll pretend we're at the supermarket. I'll name two things we see that begin with the same sound. If I say *banana, butter,* and *cheese,* which two begin with the same sound? Good. Now you name one more thing we can see at the supermarket that starts with the same sound that you hear at the beginning of *banana* and *butter.* (*bread, beef, biscuits,* etc.)"

Initial Consonant Sounds:

/s/	salt	soap	(soup, cereal, celery, strawberries)
/ch/	cherries	cheese	(chicken, chocolate, chips)
/m/	meat	muffins	(milk, macaroni, matches, mustard)
/p/	pears	potatoes	(pie, prunes, pork, peas)
/k/	corn	candy	(crackers, kale, carrots, kraut, cream)
/r/	rice	raisins	(rhubarb, raspberries, wrapping paper, rib roast)
/t/	toys	turnips	(tomatoes, tea, tamales, tangerines)

Initial and Medial Vowel Sounds:

/ă/	apples	ham	(jam, pancake flour, lamb, carrots)
/ĕ/	egg	bread	(lettuce, pepper, thread)
/ē/	cheese	meat	(coffee, tea, peanuts, cereal)
/ā/	cake	steak	(potatoes, raisins, dates, paper plates)
/ō/	oatmeal	soap	(oleo, soda, bologna, cocoa)
/ī/	ice cream	pie	(rice, pineapple, price tags, iodized salt)
/ä/	pop	olives	(boxes, lox, margarine, barley)

28. Reuben Says, Rachel Says (1-3)

Listening Experience: Hearing commands and discriminating between those to be executed and those to be ignored.

A leader is chosen; if a girl, she is Rachel; if a boy, he is Rueben. The leader stands facing the class.

The children stand. The leader commands, "Rachel says, 'Do this.'" The leader then makes a motion with hands, feet, or head, or makes a facial grimace. The children do as shown, and the leader gives another command. If the command is preceded by "Rachel (Reuben) says" the children must carry out the direction; if the command is *not* preceded by "Rachel says," the children must *not* follow the direction under penalty of sitting down for the remainder of the leader's turn.

Leaders should change after about ten commands.

The teacher may act as the first leader in order to demonstrate.

Variation:

■ The children are seated and the leader gives a series command to one child only. Example: "Reuben (Rachel) says, 'Go to the board, write your name, walk to the window, then go to your seat.' Tom Smith, do it." If the named child executes the directions correctly and if they were preceded by "Reuben (Rachel) says," he becomes the leader. If the directions are not preceded by "Reuben (Rachel) says," he stays in his seat.

Usually a series of two or three actions is sufficient. However, the difficulty of the game should be governed by the maturity of the group.

Correlate with: Lesson 18, "Follow My Directions"

29. *Think Fast (1-3)*

Listening Experiences: Hearing commands and responding quickly. Recognizing and matching sounds.

Children take turns to see who can name the greatest number of words that begin with specified consonant sounds in one minute. Other children listen to be sure   e words are acceptable.

When a child detects an error, he takes the next turn.

Again, the emphasis is on sounds, not spelling. Talk about the sound of /k/ as in *candy* and *kick*; the sound of /s/ as in *city* and *stamp*; the sound of /f/ as in *phone* and *forget*; the sound of /h/ as in *who* and *horse*.

30. Guess Who (1-3)

Listening Experience: Hearing a description, selecting clues, and identifying the person described.

Start the activity by saying, for example, "I'm thinking of a boy in this room who is always cheerful. Today I heard him offer to help someone who was having trouble with arithmetic. He has brown eyes and light brown hair. Guess who."

The child who volunteers the correct name becomes the next leader. If no one can make the correct identification, give more clues until someone names the right person. The namer then becomes the leader.

The teacher should discuss the importance of considering the feelings of others, and take care that only admirable qualities and actions are used as clues.

Variations:

■ Describe storybook characters.

■ Describe a well-known person, either from the past or a contemporary.

Correlate with: Lesson 14, "Say Something Nice about Someone"
Lesson 66, "The New Coat"
Lesson 67, "The New School"

31. Ear Sharpeners (2-3)

Listening Experience: Distinguishing between same and different initial sounds.

Ask the children to stand beside their chairs, and tell them: "I will say four words while you listen. Listen to the sound that starts the first word. When you hear a word that starts like the first word, raise your right hand. If you raise your hand for a word that doesn't start like the first word, you must sit down."

Use any of the suggested word groups below or make up your own.

1. man	milk	many	name
2. cake	near	car	came
3. dog	boy	day	deer
4. fire	fish	farm	house
5. gone	goat	plant	go
6. hat	book	house	here
7. joy	jam	juice	tomato
8. lamb	like	my	little
9. never	now	near	table
10. pet	part	puppy	lamp
11. rice	four	rat	river
12. see	sit	Celia	Jim
13. town	table	touch	city
14. wall	went	war	run
15. add	apple	ape	ant
16. egg	Edith	elf	edge
17. ice	idea	Ida	ill
18. ocean	over	open	October
19. uncle	you	us	untie
20. yogurt	yes	your	want
21. ape	ate	Amy	Annie
22. eat	egg	each	eel
23. ill	imitate	ice	important
24. October	oblong	open	occupy
25. use	Utah	us	usual

Variation:

■ Ask the children to distinguish between like and different ending sounds. Example: li<u>p</u>, ra<u>p</u>, si<u>t</u>; soa<u>p</u>, ro<u>p</u>e, ro<u>s</u>e.

32. Which Way? (2-3)

Listening Experience: Recognizing and executing valid commands involving compass directions.

This game is played much as "Reuben Says, Rachel Says," except that the leader uses compass directions in the commands: "Reuben says, 'Turn north'"; "Rachel says, 'Face east'"; "Reuben says, 'Point northwest.'" Children should respond only to commands preceded by "Reuben (Rachel) says."

Children who respond to an incorrect command or who respond with a wrong direction must sit down until the next leader is chosen. A leader should give about ten commands.

If the class prefers, the leader may use his or her own name instead of "Reuben" or "Rachel."

Correlate with: Lesson 70, "Emergency"

33. Opposites (2-3)

Listening Experience: Recognizing words of opposite meaning in spoken statements.

One or the Other

Ask the children to listen for opposites in each sentence. Alert them to the fact that some sentences have two pairs of opposites.

1. The <u>city</u> is a <u>noisy</u> place, but it's <u>quiet</u> in the <u>country</u>.
2. A lion is a <u>big</u> animal, but a cat is a <u>little</u> one.
3. Carl likes to tease; when his little brother <u>cries</u>, Carl <u>laughs</u> at him.
4. I <u>lost</u> a dime this <u>morning</u> but I <u>found</u> it this <u>evening</u>.
5. The teacher said, "If you have questions, <u>ask</u> and I'll try to <u>answer</u> them for you."
6. Which do you like best—<u>sweet</u> pickles or <u>sour</u> pickles?
7. The <u>red</u> light means <u>stop</u>; the <u>green</u> light means <u>go</u>.
8. In <u>summer</u> the days are <u>long</u>; in <u>winter</u>, they're <u>short</u>.
9. <u>Inside</u> the house on a winter day
   I'm <u>warm</u> and nice.
   <u>Outside</u> the house on a winter day
   I'm <u>cold</u> as ice.

34. One or the Other (2-3)

Listening Experience: Understanding alternative commands and responding quickly and accurately.

The children stand in a circle. The leader is in the center with a rubber ball. As he tosses the ball to a player he calls either "Animal!" or "Bird!" The person who catches the ball must respond by naming some animal or bird, as called for, before the leader can count to 15. The player who succeeds in naming a bird or animal within the required time takes the leader's place. Any animal or bird may be named only once during the game.

If, after ten or twelve turns the children are struggling to think of bird and animal names, start the game over using one of the variations.

Note: Of course, birds are also animals. If you wish to be more precise, and if the children are familiar with the term, substitute *mammal* for *animal*.

Variations:

■ Use other categories, such as: fruits and vegetables; days of the week and months of the year (correlate with Lesson 26, "The Seasons"); animal, vegetable, or mineral.

35. What Else? (2-3)

Listening Experience: Hearing, remembering, and expanding a sequence of statements.

The first player says, "When I went camping I took a tent." The second player repeats what the first has said and adds another item, as: "When I went camping I took a tent and a _____" (perhaps flashlight or canteen). Each successive player begins with "When I went camping" and names the items in the same order before adding one of his own.

When a child is unable to remember the sequence or add an item, he selects a volunteer who continues the game.

If the group is large it is advisable to stop the first camping trip and start a second and even a third.

Variations:

- When I went to the zoo I saw a _____ (series of zoo animal and birds).
- I can spell _____ (series of words from recent spelling lessons).
- When I got up this morning, I _____ (series of actions in a sequence).

Correlate with: Lesson 19, "At the Supermarket"

36. Word Shuttle (2-3)

Listening Experience: Hearing words spelled. Spelling words beginning with specified letters.

The class divides into two equal lines facing each other. The teacher designates the first child to play. He spells any word he chooses, e.g., *kitten.* The child directly opposite him in the other line must spell a word which begins with the last letter of *kitten,* e.g., *not.* The second child in the first line then spells a word that begins with *t.* The spelling continues in this manner as words are shuttled back and forth from line to line.

A word may be spelled no more than once during a game. A player sits down if he misspells a word, or repeats a word already spelled, or is unable to think of a word. When all the children in one line are down, the other group wins. If they wish, the remaining group members can continue spelling until the last child left standing is the individual winner.

37.   What Am I Thinking Of? (2-3)

Listening Experience: Using rhymes for clues to
identify words.

The object of this game is to find a word that fits the clues given by the leader. The clues pertain to sound and meaning. For example, the leader might say, "I'm thinking of a kind of tree that rhymes with *smoke*. What is it?" (*oak*) Or, "I'm thinking of a kind of building that rhymes with *mouse*. What is it?" (*house*)

The child who answers correctly becomes leader and presents the next riddle. If a child's answer satisfies the requirements of the question, it is considered correct, even if it is not what the leader had in mind.

It's a good idea to give the children a few minutes' time before starting the game to prepare one or two of these rhyming riddles. You may want to act as leader for the first few times, especially with younger children. Here are a few suggested rhyming riddles:

I'm thinking of a color that rhymes with *chew*. (blue)

I'm thinking of an animal that rhymes with *hat*. (cat, bat, rat)

I'm thinking of a flower that rhymes with *hilly*. (lily)

I'm thinking of a part of our 24-hour day that rhymes with *fight*. (night)

I'm thinking of something to eat that rhymes with *lake*. (steak, cake)

I'm thinking of a dark color that rhymes with *Jack*. (black)

I'm thinking of a piece of furniture that rhymes with *hair*. (chair)

I'm thinking of an ocean animal that rhymes with *pail*. (whale, snail)

38. Making Riddles (2-3)

Listening Experience: Hearing a group of clues and
identifying the described object.

Give each child a slip of paper on which you have written
the name of an object he or she will use in making a riddle.
Use the names of animals, fruits and vegetables, or any objects your children are sure to be familiar with. Ask the children to take a few minutes to think of three or four clues which
would help the others guess the identity of their individual
objects.

One of the children is chosen to begin the game by giving
one clue to his object. If no one can guess, he gives another
clue, and continues to give clues until the riddle is solved or
the group gives up. Here is an example:

I'm a machine. People use me in their houses, in their cars,
and outdoors. You can turn me on or off. I can be pretty big or
so small that you can carry me in your pocket. I'm a radio.

Here are a few suggestions of objects for riddle-making:
Machines: TV set, clock, auto, truck, airplane, computer
Animals: camel, kangaroo, giraffe, snake, lion, dog, cat, mouse
Birds: sparrow, turkey, duck, parrot, canary, eagle, pigeon,
owl
Buildings: post office, police station, fire station, school,
house, skyscraper
People: mother, father, other relatives, teacher, doctor, mail-
man, salesperson
Fruits and vegetables: pineapple, orange, watermelon, sweet
corn, pumpkin, onion, cocoanut

Correlate with.   Lesson 25, "Riddles"

39.   Go On (2-3)

Listening Experience: Hearing a portion of an unfamiliar narrative and creating an appropriate continuation.

The leader begins an original story. After a few sentences the leader stops and points to another child, saying, "Go on." The second child adds a few sentences, stops, points to another, and says, "Go on."

The story continues in this manner until a satisfactory ending is reached.

Variation:

■ Retelling a familiar story in the same manner.

Correlate with: Lesson 68, "Telling Tales"

40.   What Would You Leave Out? (3)

Listening Experience: Hearing and rejecting nonessential information

Explain to the children that you will read them some paragraphs and that in each paragraph there is a sentence that does not keep to the topic. Direct the children to listen for the nonessential statement as you read each paragraph. Here are two examples:

Most children would like to have an animal as a pet. The most common pets are cats and dogs, but sometimes a horse or a cow or a pig can be a pet. Birthdays are fun. Hamsters and rabbits also make good pets.

Maria and Peggy are good friends. They play games, jump rope, ride their bikes, and go to Brownies together. Maria's dog, Tuffy, can run very fast. Maria and Peggy walk to school together and visit each other on Saturday.

41. One Minute! (3)

Listening Experience: Hearing a category named and naming items that belong in it.

Explain to the children that each player will have one minute to list five objects that belong in a category which the player will be given. Name the category and start timing while the player calls the objects.

Children who are successful in beating the clock put their names on the chalkboard.

Here are some suggestions for categories:

things that fly	birds	flowers
musical instruments	dogs	trees
domestic animals	makes of cars	fish
wild animals	vegetables	boys' names
cities of the world	fruit	girls' names

SECTION 2

Poems and Rhymes

42.   The Owl (K-1)

Listening Experiences: Hearing and enjoying a poem, then participating in discussion about it.

Read the poem, or have a child read it.

> Old Mr. Owl has big round eyes
> Which make this bird look very wise.
> He never flies in sunshine bright,
> But on dark days or in the night.
>
> Silently he looks for food,
> And hunts fat mice in field and wood.
> While in the nest are owlets two,
> And Mrs. Owl calls, "Who, whoo, whooo?"
>
> Even though owls have big round eyes
> Which make them look extremely wise,
> About all they know how to do
> Is hunt for food and call, "Who, whooo?"

Discussion and Oral Exercises:
- At what time of day do owls hunt for food?
- Why don't they fly in bright sunlight?
- Are they smarter than other birds?
- Why do people think owls look wise?
- Can you sound like an owl?
- Which word does not rhyme in each line?

1.	eyes	wise	fly
2.	bright	owl	night
3.	two	who	howl
4.	who	shoe	call

Correlate with: Lesson 5, "Where Are the Owlets?"

43. *Completing Rhymes (K-2)*

Listening Experience: Hearing a sentence and providing a rhyming word that fits the rhythm and context.

Read sentences like the following and ask the children to complete them with a rhyming word.

Pamela said, "The sky is blue and my eyes are _____." (too)

John said, "It's a sunny day, let's go out and _____." (play)

Jane said, "Our baby can walk and soon she'll _____." (talk)

Jimmy said, "It's so much fun to play in the _____." (sun)

Donna said, "My father and mother are with my _____." (brother)

Paul said. "I'm going to look at my picture _____." (book)

Mark said, "Hall is my last name, and my sister's is the _____." (same)

Anne said, "A giraffe is tall, but a squirrel is _____." (small)

Oral Exercise:

■ "Listen while I say two words that rhyme. Then you tell me some words that rhyme with them."

blue, too	(you, shoe, stew)
day, play	(say, clay, away)
walk, talk	(chalk, hawk, stalk)
fun, sun	(bun, run, done, gun)
look, book	(cook, hook, took)
name, same	(came, lame, tame)
tall, small	(ball, hall, call)
show, toe	(bow, crow, sew, go)

44. The Steam Goblin (K-2)

Listening Experience: Participating in choral speaking
                          and discussing context.

Read this poem several times so that the children can enjoy
it and get to know it, then explain what each group will do in
the choral speaking. Aim for fun rather than for perfection.

> *Leader:*   A steam goblin lives in our teakettle,
> *Girls:*   In our teakettle,
> *Boys:*   In our teakettle.
> *Leader:*   A steam goblin lives in our teakettle,
>   Every day in the year.
> *Girls:*   He bangs
>   And he clangs,
> *Boys:*   He bumps
>   And he thumps,
>   As he bangs on the top
>   With a leap and a hop.
> *All:*   A steam goblin lives in our teakettle,
>   Every day in the year.

Discussion and Oral Exercises:

■ Are goblins real? Name some other scary things that aren't
real. (ghosts, witches, monsters, etc.)
■ What causes the banging in the teakettle when the heat is
turned on high? Have you ever heard it? Did you know what
it was?

Variation:

■ Instead of dividing the group into girls and boys, you can
divide numerically, with each half of the group taking one
part.

Correlate with: Lesson 5, "Where Are the Owlets?"
Lesson 46, "A Halloween Scare"
Lesson 47, "A Haunted House"
Lesson 55, "The Grunch Wants Lunch"

45.   *Old Mrs. Spider (K-3)*

Listening Experiences: Hearing a poem. Perceiving words
of opposite meanings.

Read the poem several times for the children's enjoyment
and familiarization. For kindergarten children this may be all
that is possible. Older children can be asked to identify the
words of opposite meaning in most lines or pairs of lines. For
such an activity, the poem should be reread somewhat slowly,
either by you or by various children who read well. The
antonyms are underlined.

Old Mrs. Spider caught young Buzzy Fly
Near the ceiling, in her web so high.
Old Mrs. Spider has sharp, black eyes
To find dull insects who aren't very wise.
Old Mrs. Spider runs up and down the wall.
With her eight legs she's not afraid she'll fall.
Over and under her sticky web is spun,
Thin bugs and fat bugs, she gets them every one.
Old Mrs. Spider is busy day and night,
Catching many insects in darkness or daylight.

Oral Exercise:
■ Name the opposites of these words, all of them and their
opposites in the poem: *young, sharp, down, under, fat,
night, daylight.*

Correlate with: Lesson 33, "Opposites"
Lesson 50, "Hopping with Harvey"

---

46. A Halloween Scare (K-3)

Listening Experiences: Listening to a longer poem.
Detecting rhyming words.

Read the poem to the children once, then have one or two children read it aloud. In this way they can enjoy it and become familiar with it before they single out the rhyming words.

> Halloween is lots of fun
> With witches, cats, and ghosts,
> And yet it kind of scares me—
> But my friend Jerry boasts
> That he's not scared of those things
> Because they are not real,
> And he's afraid of nothing that
> He can't reach out and feel.
>
> Two nights ago, on Halloween,
> We went for trick or treat,
> And people filled our bags full
> Of yummy things to eat.
> Then down a street that had no lights
> Jerry said, "Let's go!"
> But what we were to meet there
> Brave Jerry did not know.
>
> For on that scary street
> There was a willow tree,

And as we hurried past it,
Something jumped out at me!
Oh! I was scared! That I'll admit.
But my friend began to run!
Then we both felt pretty foolish—
It was Jerry's brother having fun.

Discussion and Oral Exercises:
- Jerry is called "brave Jerry" in the poem. Does it mean that Jerry really was brave?
- Have you had any scary Halloween experiences?
- What words in the poem rhyme with these words?
     roasts   peel   seat   blow   he   sun

Correlate with: Lesson 17, "A Halloween Game"
                     Lesson 44, "The Steam Goblin"
                     Lesson 47, "A Haunted House"

47. A Haunted House (K-3)

Listening Experiences: Listening to a poem. Hearing a
                            word picture and visualizing it.

Before you start to read the poem, suggest that the children close their eyes and try to see a picture of the haunted house. Tell them to keep their picture a secret. After the reading, ask the children to draw a picture of the haunted house as they saw it.

Ghosts afloatin' through the doors,
Witches creepin' down the stair,
Boards acreakin' in the floors,
Bats aflyin' in the air.

Spider webs hang from the ceilin',
Dark old rooms with paint apeelin',
Broken, dirty windows, too—
Say! I don't like this place, do you?

Discussion:

■ Compare and discuss the drawings from the point of view of how people "see" things.

Correlate with: Lesson 17, "A Halloween Game"
Lesson 44, "The Steam Goblin"
Lesson 45, "Old Mrs. Spider"
Lesson 46, "A Halloween Scare"

48. Butterflies (K-3)

Listening Experiences: Listening to a poem and perceiving rhyming words. Visualizing from the verbal expression.

Read the poem to the children; let them enjoy it and familiarize themselves with it. Reread it as necessary for the discussion and exercises.

The butterfly with gauzy wings
Spends pleasant, lazy hours
Flying, dipping, soaring, sipping
Honey from the flowers.

Away among the leafy trees
He flutters up and down,
Gliding, floating, gently riding
Over field and town.

Discussion and Oral Exercises:

■ Suggest that the children close their eyes while you reread the poem. Ask them to try to picture a butterfly in flight.

■ Use a children's encyclopedia article to discuss the life cycle of butterflies.

■ Reread the poem as children listen for rhyming words. Ask: "What words in the poem rhyme with these words?"

sings   showers   bees   clown

■ A small group may like to pretend they are butterflies, flitting and gliding about the room as you and the rest of the children repeat the poem.

Correlate with: Lesson 64, "Changing Plans"

49. Clouds at Play (K-3)

Listening Experiences: Listening to a poem; perceiving rhyming words. Visualizing and imagining from verbal expression.

Read the poem for enjoyment and familiarization. Then reread it for the discussion and exercises.

Fluffy clouds go drifting by
Up there in the bright blue sky.
Sometimes fast and sometimes slow,
The wind shoves them to and fro.

Now together, floating free,
Pictures up there I can see.
Castles, ships, and dragons too,
All come sailing into view.

Clouds at Play

Hopping with Harvey

Giraffes and elephants so tall,
Birds and beasts both great and small,
All go drifting 'cross the sky
Along the air roads there on high.

Slowly then, they disappear,
Pieces drifting far and near
As they twist and sail away
Joining other clouds at play.

Discussion and Oral Exercises:
- Ask: "Have you ever tried to see pictures in the clouds? Tell about it."
- Ask: "What makes the clouds move?"
- Reread the poem as children listen for rhyming words. (In this poem, the first and second lines, and the third and fourth lines, rhyme.)

50. Hopping with Harvey (K-3)

Listening Experience: Hearing a long narrative poem and recalling information from it.

Harvey is an insect,
A grasshopper quite small,
Who often goes exploring
Where garden plants grow tall.

So Harvey jumped about
One summer afternoon,
Searching for adventure
Which he found very soon.

He jumped into a garden
Right there beside the road.
The garden was the home of
A fat but hungry toad.

The hungry toad liked insects—
He ate them every day
For breakfast, lunch, and dinner—
They seldom got away.

Mosquitoes, flies, or hoppers,
He'd eat them, every one,
For gobbling juicy insects
Was his idea of fun.

He'd hide behind a plant,
Then with his sticky tongue
He'd catch the insect—fast!
His tongue flicked: "Zing, zang, zung!"

Harvey landed on the lettuce
And he began to sing.
Then right before his eyes
Something flashed zing! zing!

Thump! Kerthump! went Harvey's heart.
He quickly jumped away,
And hid beneath a lettuce leaf,
Too worried, now, to play.

And then, while Harvey trembled,
A big bluebottle fly
Came buzzing by and landed
On the beets nearby.

Zing! Zang! Zung! went Old Toad's tongue.
And then he went Crunch! Crunch!
He gobbled up that poor old fly—
It was a tasty lunch.

Harvey's heart still went thump, thump.
He whispered, "Now I see.
Old Toad got Mr. Bluebottle
And he almost got me.

"I greatly fear he still is near,
And he will soon be back,
I do not wish to be his dish,
Or even a light snack.

"I'll just hide here and go to sleep,
In the morning I'll feel fine."
So we'll leave Harvey now
Till tomorrow, about nine.

•　•　•　•　•

When Harvey woke next morning
It was a cloudy day,
But the air was soft and pleasant
So he went out to play.

High upon a cornstalk
He saw a katydid.
It took sharp eyes to see her
Whenever Katy hid.

"Hi, Katy!" he called shrilly.
"Come on! Let's go and play!
You ought to be real happy
For it's a cloudy day!"

Now Katy was quite shy,
She didn't like the sun,
So nights and cloudy days
Were the times when she had fun.

"I'm ready," Katy trilled.
"But what is there to do?"
"Let's go adventuring," Harvey said,
"Let's go and see what's new."

The two friends hopped along
And soon came to a marsh.
Then, from a willow tree,
There came a call so harsh.

"Caw! Caw! Caw! Caw! Caw!"
Old Blacky Crow called out.
Shy Katy's six legs trembled
And Harvey gave a shout.

"Katy! Katy! Jump! Jump quick!"
And Katy did jump fast.
She didn't stop for questions
Until the danger passed.

When Harvey called to Katy
They'd both jumped very high,
And now the two were clinging
To a small bush nearby.

Below them in the marsh grass
There lurked an old bullfrog,
Just waiting for young insects
To come close to his log.

There, in the slippery mud
The frog, so big and green
Was croaking out his angry threats.
To them, he seemed quite mean.

"You two spry young hoppers
Think that you're mighty wise,
But one fine day, I'll get you!
I'll take you by surprise!

"Some day you just won't see me,
Then I'll have a good lunch,
For there is nothing better
Than juicy bugs to munch!"

Old Frog certainly looked cross,
His shiny eyes just glared.
The little insects trembled
For they were badly scared.

But then, not far away
The grass began to shake,
And creeping close to Mr. Frog
Was the head of Mr. Snake!

Across a log he slithered
Close to the frog he came,
Who still was boasting loudly
When Harvey yelled his name.

"Jump, Mr. Frog, jump! Get away!
Quick! Get away from here!
Someone's near you on the log—
Someone that you fear!"

Kerplunk! Kerplunk! went Mr. Frog.
You should have seen him dive!
"Thanks, hopper," he was heard to say,
"He won't get me alive!"

The garter snake—that's what he was—
Couldn't believe his eyes—
For Harvey's sudden yell
Had taken him by surprise.

"You've ruined my meal, you foolish thing,
That frog was not your friend—
He'll soon forget you saved his life
And then you'll meet your end."

Then Katy called to Harvey,
"Let's get away from here!
I don't think I like this marsh,
There's just too much to fear!"

"It keeps us hopping," Harvey said,
"To stay away from danger,
Too often in our life, it seems
That danger is no stranger."

Down from the bush they jumped
And hopped away toward home,
Back to their cozy haystack
No more that day to roam.

Discussion and Oral Exercises:

■ If the group shows interest, "Hopping with Harvey" may
be used as a springboard to learning about similarities and
contrasts in the life cycles of animals, birds, and insects.
■ Ask children to recall the animals, birds, and insects that

are mentioned in this story poem. (grasshopper, toad, mosquitoes, flies, katydid, crow, bullfrog, garter snake)
- Ask: "What part of the story poem did you like best?"
- Discuss: Are animals (including birds and insects) bad when they eat other animals?

Correlate with: Lesson 45, "Old Mrs. Spider"
Lesson 48, "Butterflies"
Lesson 63, "Changing Plans"
Lesson 55, "The Grunch Wants Lunch"

51. Silly Rhymes (1-3)

Listening Experience: Hearing internal rhymes in
a poem.

A hawk can't talk,
A fox can't box,
A calf can't laugh,
But a dog can jog.

A fly can't cry,
A bug can't hug,
Pigs don't wear wigs,
But a girl can whirl.

A sheep can't weep,
A cow can't bow,
Nor a flea drink tea,
But a bee can see.

These thoughts are new.
Do you think they're true?

Discussion and Oral Exercises:
- Reread the verses a line at a time and ask the children to find the two rhyming words in each line (with the exception of the last two lines).
- Ask: "What is a hawk? A flea? A calf?"
- Ask: "What does it mean to jog? To box? To weep? Show us."
- Read the poem again without interruption for further enjoyment of humor and rhyme.

Correlate with: Lesson 54, "The Animal Picnic"

52. Do They Rhyme? (1-3)

Listening Experience: Discriminating between rhymes and non-rhymes.

Read each horizontal line of five words after directing the children to listen for the one word which does not rhyme. Children may call out the non-rhyming word after they have heard the five words.

1. bird	word	girl	heard	third
2. man	toy	boy	joy	Roy
3. gun	fun	sun	bun	hop
4. any	boy	many	penny	Jenny
5. fire	tree	three	me	see
6. cow	pow	how	this	now
7. fight	lamp	light	sight	bright
8. crew	blue	kerchoo	ouch	canoe

Oral Exercise:
- Think of more words that rhyme with the words in each line.

53. Rabbitnapping (1-3)

Listening Experience: Listening to a narrative poem and
discussing its content.

The sun was warm one bright spring day
When Mite, the dog, went out to play.
She barked and jumped and tried some tricks
As she chased rabbits, mice and chicks.

Then all at once she saw a sight
Which made her feel such great delight:
A nest of bunnies with bright eyes
And twitching noses — quite a prize.

For Mite loved babies — any kind!
Her short tail wagged as through her mind
There flashed a thought — and then it grew —
She'd add a baby to her two.

Mite didn't wait. She headed south
With a small bunny in her mouth.
Then just before she reached her door
She met Janice going to the store.

"Why, Mite," said Janice, "what have you done?
Where did you find this little one?"
But Mite ran on, she didn't wait,
Across the field and through the gate

With Janice running far behind
Calling to her, "You've lost your mind!
That bunny's wild! He will not eat
Your puppy biscuits and your meat!"

Mite put the baby with her two,
And then gave him a bone to chew.
His small nose twitched, his long ears turned,
'Cause gnawing bones he hadn't learned.

The pups rushed up and touched his nose.
They smelled his fur and licked his toes,
While Mother Mite wagged her short tail
As though to say, "My plan won't fail."

Then Mite called to her family,
"It's time to eat, now come to me."
The hungry pups came running fast
For neither one wished to be last.

And as they nursed, the bunny's eyes
Looked bright and shiny and so wise:
He knew at once what he should do,
And so he joined the puppies too.

Then Janice laughed, "You funny Mite
I'm sure you don't know it's not right
To rabbitnap this baby here.
I like him too. He is a dear.

"But I can't let you make a habit
Of stealing babes from Mother Rabbit.
She will be worried, I suppose,
So when he's finished, back he goes!"

Discussion and Oral Exercises:

■ Ask: Why did Mite take the baby bunny? (third verse)
    Do you think Mite knew the mother rabbit would miss
    her baby?

How did the baby rabbit know the way to get milk from Mite? (tenth verse)

What did Janice mean when she said Mite rabbit-napped the baby?

■ Here is a series of statements for true-or-false anwers. The children may raise right hands for *true* and left hands for *false*.

Mite found the bunny on a cloudy day. (false)
Mite liked to chase rabbits and mice. (true)
Mite wouldn't chase chickens. (false)
Mite chased the baby rabbit home. (false)
Rabbits like to chew on bones. (false)
The two puppies didn't like the baby bunny. (false)
Janice is a human; Mite is a dog. (true)
Janice said she would return the bunny to its mother. (true)
Eyes, wise, and *prize* are rhyming words. (true)
Rabbit and *habit* are rhyming words. (true)
Nose and *tail* are rhyming words. (false)

Correlate with: Lesson 61, "Puppysitting"

54. The Animal Picnic (2-3)

Listening Experiences: Listening to nonsense verses and discussing the vocabulary. Perceiving internal and external rhymes. Enjoying humorous fantasy.

One day by the sea
I saw a flea and a bee
Sitting high in a tree.

I saw a humpback whale
Swish his slippery tail
In a water pail,

While a tabby cat,
Who's an acrobat
Twirled a lariat.

Then a bear with no hair
Rode on to the fair
As he ate a spare pear.

And a pretty pink pig
With a curly wig
Danced a jig.

I saw a hairy yak
With a pack on his back
Sitting on a tack,

And I caught a spunky
Ring-tailed monkey
Stealing honey from a donkey,

While a wily skunk
Hid inside a trunk
Near a camper's bunk.

Then a grand crocodile
Brushed his teeth with a file
To improve his smile,

While a proud billy goat
Fell kerplunk from his boat
And soaked his new coat.

And an electric eel
Cooked her family a meal
With great vigor and zeal.

Then, with teeth like a saw
Some beavers did gnaw
Tree bark for coleslaw.

Nearby, in the park,
I heard a puppy bark
As he teased a shark.

A koala bear in a tree
Rubbed salve on his knee,
For he was stung by a bee.

I saw a shivering lizard
Pretend he was a wizard
In a freezing blizzard,

Then an Angora cat
Lost her frilly French hat
As she chased a rude rat.

And a silly young beagle
Tried to fly like an eagle
'Cause he wished to look regal.

I saw a smart ladybug
Put out a fire in her rug
With milk from a jug.

Then they all said "Goodbye
Till the next Fourth of July"
Do you think I would lie?

Discussion and Oral Exercises:

■ Which of all the animals mentioned in this poem did you like best?
Have you ever been to a funny picnic?
Were there some animals you had never heard of before?

■ Discuss the following animals; use data from children's encyclopedias.

humpback whale	ring-tailed monkey
crocodile	koala bear
electric eel	beagle
beaver	eagle
yak	bee

■ Discuss the meaning of the following words:

wily　lariat　jig　spunky　salve　vigor
gnaw　wizard　zeal　improve　regal　fully

■ Reread lines showing inside (internal) rhymes: verse 1, line 2; verse 4, lines 1 and 3; verse 6, line 2.

■ Encourage children to make up more verses for "The Animal Picnic." This can be done as an oral group activity, with children suggesting lines that you write on the chalkboard.

Correlate with: Lesson 51, "Silly Rhymes"

55. The Grunch Wants Lunch (2-3)

Listening Experiences: Participating in choral speaking. Discussing context. Enjoying rhythm, fantasy, and humor.

Leader: There was an old grunch who wanted some lunch.
Group: The grunch wanted some lunch? (*amazement*)
Leader: So he snitched a pie before you could wink your eye.

The Animals' Picnic

The Grunch Wants Lunch

Group: Before you could wink your eye?
Leader: Next he gobbled a frog right off of a log.
Group: A frog off of a log?
Leader: And a sleepy snake that lived in a lake.
Group: The snake lived in a lake?
Leader: Then, some carpenter ants, all doing a dance.
Group: Ants doing a dance?
Leader: So now the old grunch had had a big lunch.
Group: The grunch had a *big* lunch.
Leader: But something funny took place in his tummy.
Group: Something funny in his tummy? (*wonder*)
Leader: The ants ate the pie 'fore you'd wink an eye.
Group: The ants ate the pie?
Leader: The frog ate the ants, still doing their dance.
Group: The frog ate the ants?
Leader: The snake ate the frog who'd lived on a log.
Group: The snake ate the frog?
Leader: But the grunch hiccuped and then—the snake was outside again!
Group: The snake was outside again? (*amazement*)
Leader: And the poor old grunch still hadn't had lunch.
Group: The grunch hadn't had lunch. (*slowly*)

Discussion and Exercises:

■ How do you think the grunch looked? Draw a picture of him. (It is expected that the children will visualize the grunch in widely differing ways.)
■ What did you like best in this poem? Could it be true?
■ Discuss carpenter ants, using information from a children's encyclopedia.
■ Have children say the poem in chorus, always striving for enjoyment rather than perfection.

Correlate with: Lesson 44, "The Steam Goblin"

56. Little Words in Big Words (2-3)

Listening Experiences: Hearing rhyming couplets and
thinking about compound words.
Perceiving rhyming words.

After you have read the verses once for enjoyment, reread
them one couplet at a time, directing the children to listen for
words made of two smaller words put together (compounds),
and rhyming words. The compounds are underlined.

A bluebird was singing
While Jan was swinging.

Jim wore his raincoat
When he rode on the boat.

Gwen has a flashlight
That is extra bright.

The baby was told
That a snowman is cold.

The firemen's red truck
Almost hit a duck.

Dad said he would take
Our sailboat to the lake.

Our parrot needs
Some sunflower seeds.

Many trucks every day
Drive on the <u>highway</u>.

Discussion and Oral Exercise:
■ Have the children think of other compound words. Since the spelling of compound words varies—some are closed (*fairground*), some open (*fair copy*) and some hyphenated (*fair-trade*), accept any compound regardless of its spelling.

57. Talking in Rhyme (3)

Listening Experience: Recalling rhyming words and using them in verse statements.

Begin by saying to the children:

Let's talk in rhyme
For a time.
I wonder if you
Can think of a few?

The children should then have a short time to think. They likely will make such rhymes as:

It's fun to play
On a nice day.

I saw a bug
On the rug.

If the children find this exercise difficult, you might put

several "rhyme families" on the chalkboard to help them in finding rhyming words. Here are a few suggestions:

> bent, cent, dent, lent . . .
> ate, bait, date, fate, freight . . .
> coop, hoop, loop . . .
> by, die, guy, high . . .
> able, cable, fable, label, Mabel . .
> bum, crumb, dumb, drum . . .

SECTION **3**

Stories and Storytelling

58. Little Fellah (K-3)

Listening Experience: Enjoyment in listening to fiction.

Grandfather Davis stopped the car. "I'll get the children," he said.

Grandmother looked into the back of the car. "Hurry," she said. "Fellah wants to get out."

As Grandfather opened the car door the children saw him and started running down the walk. Jesse was first and Althea was next. Little Whitney puffed, "Wait for me!"

Grandfather called, "We have a surprise!"

Althea and Jesse hopped up and down. "Where is the surprise?" they asked.

"Please, Grandfather," Whitney begged, "what's the surprise?"

Just then a little brown face peeped over the car door. "A chimpanzee!" Jesse yelled. "You've brought us a chimpanzee! Is it a boy or a girl?"

"It's a boy," Grandfather said, "and his name is Fellah."

Althea laughed. "He's like a baby!"

The little chimp put his face up to the window and smiled. He was wearing a little red cap and a little red jacket. When Grandfather opened the car door Fellah clapped his little brown hands and jumped out. Then he put his head on the grass and somersaulted. His cap fell off but he went on. He did the trick over and over. People in their cars slowed down so they could watch Fellah perform.

Mr. Davis called from the house, "What's going on?" Beside him on the porch, Mrs. Davis put her hands over her eyes and said, "Oh, no!"

Fellah was still turning over on the ground. Grandfather called, "We thought the children would like a new pet."

Mr. Davis looked at his wife. "Oh, no!" she said again.

All at once Boy came from behind the house. He stopped when he saw Fellah. Then he barked, "Bow-wow! Bow-wow-

wow-wow!" Fellah jumped into Jesse's arms. The children gathered around him.

Jesse said, "Boy is nice, Fellah. He won't hurt you."

Grandfather sat down on the porch. "Our friends couldn't keep Fellah because they're moving to an apartment. We thought the children would like him—if it's all right with you."

The children looked at their parents. "We want to keep him! Please, please! May we keep him? Please!" they begged.

Fellah held on to Jesse's neck. He said, "Ah-hoo, ah-hoo, ah-hoo."

Mr. Davis looked at his wife. She shrugged. "Well—we can try him for a few days."

The next morning, Mrs. Davis said, "Children, will you pull the weeds out of the flower beds?"

"Sure we will," Jesse answered. "We'll get Fellah to help." As they worked, Jesse reminded Whitney and Fellah to pull only the weeds.

"Yes, just the weeds," little Whitney answered. Fellah just smiled.

After working for a while in the warm sun the children went inside for a drink of water. Fellah, left alone, smiled again as he pulled up a flower. Then he pulled another and another and another. He put flowers under his cap and in the buttonholes of his red coat. Then he smiled and danced and sang, "Ah-hoo, ah-hoo, ah-hoo."

When Mrs. Davis came outside she saw her flowers. "Oh! You bad chimp!" she said. "What will I do with you?" She thought a minute, then she said, "You must sit on a chair!" She took Fellah into the house and put him in Whitney's old high chair. "Sit there!" she said.

Fellah barked, "R-r-rhow! R-r-rhow! R-r-rhow!" He banged the tray with his fists and he screamed and kicked. The children ran to him.

Mrs. Davis said, "He must sit there. You go outside and play and I'll go out and hang up the wash." As soon as Mrs. Davis went out, Fellah stopped screaming. He waited. When Mrs. Davis came inside with the empty clothes basket he slipped out of the door.

In a little while Jesse called, "Mother! Come here!"

The wet clothes and sheets were hanging high up in the apple tree. Fellah smiled down from the top of the tree. Then he picked green apples and let them fall. Bump! Bump! One fell right on Mrs. Davis's head. As she rubbed the hurt place she snapped, "I've had enough! We'll give him to the man in the pet store!"

The children cried, "No! No! We want to keep Fellah!" Jesse and Althea started to climb up the tree. "We'll get the clothes," they called.

Jesse and Althea dropped the clothes from the tree while Whitney put them into the basket. Their mother was cross as she went into the house to do the wash over again.

The next day, when he was home from work, Mr. Davis started to paint the garage. But when he went into the house to answer a phone call, Fellah ran to the garage. He put the paint brush into the white paint. He looked around and saw a shiny green car. He brushed white paint on the doors and the windows and the wheels. He stopped a minute when he came to the cap of the gas tank. He turned and the cap came off. Fellah smiled. "Ah-hoo, ah-hoo, ah-hoo," he said softly as he peeped into the dark gas tank. Boy came and peeped in too.

Just then Mr. Davis came out of the house. First he saw the paint on the car and then he spied Fellah at the gas tank. He ran. "Stop it! Stop it!" he shouted as he caught Fellah by the arm. Boy was so scared that he ran away, his tail between his legs. Mrs. Davis and the children heard the noise and came running.

"Oh, no!" Mrs. Davis said when she saw the car.

Jesse whispered to Althea, "I know they'll give him away now."

Mr. Davis looked at his wife. "You were right. That chimp has to go!" He held Fellah out to the children. "Take him! I don't want to see him out here again!" He looked at the car and shook his head. "I'll have to clean that white paint off before it dries. I hope I have enough turpentine."

Jesse took the little chimpanzee. "I'll clean him up," he said.

Mrs. Davis said, "Clean him up, put him in bed and shut the door. Then we'll know where he is!"

Fellah liked Whitney's little bed. He held the children's old teddy bear and sang, "E-e-eou, e-e-eou, e-e-eou." Soon he was sleeping.

The next day Mrs. Davis and the children got ready to go shopping. "Let's take Fellah," Althea said.

"Well . . ." her mother said. "I don't know."

"Please, Mom," Althea begged. "He'll be good."

"Well, all right," her mother said, "if you children will look after him."

In the shopping mall Althea took Fellah's hand as they walked along. "You're nice," she said. He looked up at her and smiled. The boys went into the dime store and Althea and her mother went into another store to look at clothes.

In a little while Althea was in a fitting room trying on skirts and dresses with her mother's help. Fellah, meanwhile, peeped under the partition into the next fitting room. A woman was trying on a red dress. Fellah pulled on the lady's shoe. She screamed and ran out of the fitting room with the dress over her head, shouting, "A big hairy monster took hold of my shoe! I saw his hand! It was terrible! Oh, I have to sit down!" The red dress was still over her head.

Mrs. Davis, Althea, and a very innocent-looking Fellah came out. The store manager laughed. "Is this the big monster you saw?"

The woman shouted, "Someone help me out of this dress! I'll never come into this store again!"

Mrs. Davis went to help the angry woman. "We're sorry that Fellah frightened you. He really is harmless."

Althea said, "We're very sorry."

Fellah just smiled and said, "Ah-hoo, ah-hoo, ah-hoo."

After they came home the children played outside while Fellah caught grasshoppers in the bushes beside the garage. Then he ran into the kitchen where a pot of soup was on the stove. He climbed on a chair and dropped something into the soup. He smiled and sang, "Ah-hoo, ah-hoo, ah-hoo."

That night at dinner Althea suddenly screamed, "There's a grasshopper in my soup!" Everyone looked at Fellah. He banged his high chair tray with his spoon and smiled. Then he went back to eating his mashed potatoes and carrots. Mr. and Mrs. Davis looked at each other.

"That settles it," Mr. Davis said. "We've given him a fair trial, but he's too much bother. Tomorrow we'll give him to the man in the pet store. Someone will buy him and give him a good home."

"Please, please, can't we keep him?" the children asked.

Mrs. Davis shook her head. "Daddy is right. He has to go." The children started to cry. Even Fellah looked sad.

In the night Fellah woke up. He smelled something. He ran to the kitchen and then to the boys' room. He pulled Jesse's hand, but Jesse didn't wake up. He ran to Althea's room and jumped on her bed. He pulled her hair but she pushed him away. The smell was getting stronger. Fellah was afraid. He ran to Whitney's bed and pulled on his arm, but the little boy went on sleeping.

Fellah ran back to the kitchen. Something red was coming out of the paper basket. Fire! He could see fire! He ran fast to Mr. and Mrs. Davis's room. He jumped on the bed and cried, "Ah-hoo! Ah-hoo!"

"Go away!" Mr. Davis said.

Mrs. Davis sat up. "I smell smoke!" she said. "There's a fire in the house!" She jumped out of bed.

Fellah ran to the kitchen and Mr. and Mrs. Davis followed. They splashed water on the burning paper basket as the children came running.

Mrs. Davis gasped, "This smoke! Help me open the doors and windows!"

When it was all over they sat down to rest. Mrs. Davis said, "There's really not much harm done — just smoke and a ruined plastic paper basket." She paused, and then said softly, "Fellah probably saved our lives."

Mr. Davis nodded. "You're right," he said.

Jesse and Althea jumped up. "Can we keep him?"

"Can we? Can we?" Whitney cried.

Mr. and Mrs. Davis looked at one another. She nodded. He smiled. "We'll keep him," Mr. Davis said.

The children were so happy they danced around the room. Fellah sang, "Ah-hoo, ah-hoo, ah-hoo," as he danced with the children.

Discussion and Oral Exercises:

■ What part of the story did you like best?

■ Do you think this story could happen? (Children likely would enjoy a discussion of the high intelligence of chimpanzees.)

■ Would you like a pet chimpanzee? Would you be willing to train him?

■ How would your parents feel about having a pet like Fellah?

59. Is It True? (K-3)

Listening Experiences: Discriminating between plausible and implausible story material. Recognizing and enjoying fantasy.

Tell the children that you will read (or tell) a story containing a series of statements, of which only some are believable. You will pause briefly at the end of each sentence and the children will raise their hands if they consider the statement not likely to happen. Here is an example:

One day I started downtown. I saw a group of children playing on the sidewalk. It was three o'clock in the afternoon and time that all children should be in bed for the night. But the boys were playing catch and the girls were jumping rope. I walked on. A cat was sitting on a branch above the sidewalk

Is It True?

Mickey Mole

while a dog stood below and barked at her. Suddenly the dog raced up the trunk of the tree after the cat. A man came out to call the dog.

When I got downtown I saw the people walking on their hands. Since I was walking on my feet, I felt very strange and different. I went into the supermarket and bought a new car. It was four o'clock in the afternoon as I started home and the stars were shining brightly. All of the cars on the street except mine were going backward.

My car windows were open, for it was very warm. A robin flew in carrying a baby bird. She sat on the steering wheel. I put them out of the window and they flew away with the mother still carrying the baby bird in her beak.

Then I woke up. I had had a dream.

Variation:

■ In second and third grades, children may raise their right hands for plausible statements and their left hands for implausible ones. Allow discussion to clarify any differences of opinion.

Correlate with: Lesson 44, "The Steam Goblin"
Lesson 54, "The Animal Picnic"
Lesson 55, "The Grunch Wants Lunch"

60. Mickey Mole (K-3)

Listening Experience: Receiving information and discussing it.

Mickey Mole is a small but powerful four-footed animal who lives in underground tunnels. He has strong legs, sharp, flat, claws, and a wedge-shaped head, so he can force his way through the ground and chisel away the dirt in his underground tunnels. His tiny, nearly blind eyes are protected from the dirt by thick overhanging fur. Mickey has a short hairless tail about an inch long, but his body is covered with soft, thick, bluish-gray fur.

Mickey doesn't need sharp eyes, for nearly all of his life is spent underground in his dark tunnels. But Mickey has very good ears. He can hear earthworms, beetles, and insects as they move about in the soil. His life depends upon his hearing, for Mickey eats earthworms, beetles, and insects. He is nearly always hungry, and every day he eats his own weight in his kind of food.

Mickey is a shy little animal who seldom comes above the ground. He feels safest in his underground tunnels.

Discussion and Oral Exercises:

■ After the reading, ask some or all of the following questions, depending upon the maturity of the group.

How does Mickey dig his tunnels?

How are his eyes protected from the dirt?

We heard that Mickey's head is wedge-shaped. Show us, on the chalkboard, the shape of Mickey's head. How does it help him to go through the dirt?

What is another word for dirt? (*soil* or *earth*)

How long is Mickey's tail? Describe a mole.

■ For a change of pace, have an oral true-or-false test with these statements:

Moles have very strong front legs.

Moles are nearly deaf.

Moles see very well.

Moles spend most of their lives underground.

Moles eat insects, beetles, and earthworms.

Moles have a bushy tail and reddish-brown fur.

Correlate with: Lesson 23, "Mickey Mole and Ollie Earthworm"

61. Puppy-sitting (1-3)

Listening Experiences: Enjoying a story about dogs.
Recalling information and using it
for discussion.

Mrs. Hilton took a pan of chocolate-chip cookies from the oven. The sound of yipping puppies rose from the basement.

Nancy watched her mother slide the cookies to a spatula and then to the newspaper-covered table.

"You may have some," her mother said.

As Nancy nibbled a warm cookie, Mrs. Hilton went on talking. "I don't know what we're going to do with those puppies. They're about to drive me out of my mind with their whining."

Nancy took another bite of cookie. "I know. The only time they're quiet is when they're sleeping or eating — unless it's when I'm playing with them."

Mrs. Hilton put the cookie pan in the sink. "It's too cold for them outside in the yard. I guess we'll just have to put up with their noise. Mrs. Larsen is coming over this afternoon. Would you mind playing in the basement recreation room where the puppies can see you? Then they'd be quiet and Mrs. Larsen and I could talk."

"O.K. I'll invite Ruth to come over. She likes the puppies. We'll — puppy-sit."

That afternoon the girls played downstairs. The five English sheep dog puppies, only three weeks old, seemed to be everywhere. They wobbled about on shaky legs as they explored the basement. Katy, their mother, watched them through the long grayish-white hair that hung over her eyes.

"Look at her," Nancy laughed. "She's glad, too, when they're quiet."

"Katy," Ruth said, shaking her finger at the mother dog, "you have problem children! Why don't you teach them to be quiet?"

Nancy giggled. "She looks so wise. Sometimes I think she knows what we say."

The girls started upstairs, but the puppies began their high-pitched yipping. They hurried back to the basement.

"What can I do?" Nancy said. "I promised to keep the puppies quiet while Mrs. Larsen was here."

"I know what we can do!" Ruth said. "Let's put the puppies in the doll carriage and give them a ride!"

The girls lifted all of the yipping, fat, squirming puppies into the doll carriage. The pups peered fearfully over the edge, but as soon as the girls began to push the carriage, they became very quiet. Their eyes were huge as they watched the washer, dryer, laundry tubs, and furnace go by. The carriage wheels squeaked softly under the heavy load.

Ruth giggled. "Look at Katy."

The mother dog was solemnly watching through the long hair over her eyes. In a little while she started to walk beside the girls as they took turns wheeling the doll carriage around the basement.

"Want to help wheel your babies?" Nancy asked. She raised Katy's front paws and placed them on the carriage handle. Walking carefully on her hind legs, Katy pushed the carriage.

"See how proud Katy looks!" Ruth said.

"Yes," Nancy replied. "She's just like any mother taking her children out for a ride."

That evening at dinner Nancy told her parents what Katy had done. "After we finish eating," her father said, "we'll go down and see if she'll perform for us."

As they started down the stairs, Nancy said, "Listen! That sounds like my doll-carriage wheels squeaking!" And there was Katy, pushing the carriage full of puppies around the room.

"I've never seen anything like that!" Mrs. Hilton exclaimed.

"I'm going to take a picture of this," Mr. Hilton said, and he ran upstairs to get his camera.

"Katy's smart," Nancy said. "But how did she get the puppies in the carriage?"

"Dogs and cats carry their babies by holding the little ones by their loose skin," her mother answered. "The puppies aren't very heavy, so Katy could lift them in her mouth and drop them into the carriage."

"Katy," Nancy said, "now you can take care of your puppies yourself. I won't have to keep them quiet any more! You can do your own puppy-sitting!"

Katy just looked wise and kept pushing the squeaking doll-carriage with the five quiet, happy puppies inside.

Discussion and Oral Exercises:

■ Ask comprehension questions such as the following:

What kind of dog was Katy? How many of you have seen an English sheep dog? (Discuss appearance, size, and other features. Bring in a picture, if possible.)

How many puppies did Katy have? How old were they?

Why didn't Mrs. Hilton put Katy and the puppies outside in the yard?

As Nancy and her parents went downstairs to the basement after dinner, they heard a noise. What was it?

How did Katy get her babies into the carriage?

Do you think this story could be true?

■ Encourage children to tell interesting things they have seen animals do.

■ Children may also enjoy talking about caring for pets.

Correlate with: Lesson 53, "Rabbitnapping"

62. Quite a Team (1-3)

Listening Experiences: Enjoying a story. Recalling information and using it for discussion.

Mr. MacDonald pushed back his tattered straw hat and shaded his eyes as he watched a shiny black car drive away from the fruit and vegetable stand in front of his house.

He wiped his bald head. "What am I going to do?" he thought. "If I don't work in my garden, I won't have anything to sell, but when I'm hoeing out here there isn't anyone to sell things at the stand. I need to be in two places at the same time."

A fat black and yellow bumblebee hummed as she hung above a cucumber vine; then she buzz-z-z-z-ed her way to a big orange-colored squash blossom and crawled inside.

Mr. MacDonald chopped a weed away from a cabbage plant. "I need something to tell me when people stop at the stand," he said.

Sassy, his white duck, stood quacking beside the fence. Mr. MacDonald looked at the pet. "Now why don't you quack only when people stop, instead of all the time—and for no reason at all?"

"Quack! Quack! Quack! Quack!" Sassy answered.

Suddenly Mr. MacDonald straightened up. "I've got it! I'll get a watch dog! The watch dog will bark when people stop, and I can hurry to the stand and sell my fruits and vegetables."

Taking his hoe, Mr. MacDonald started toward the garage. He stepped over rows of leaf lettuce and head lettuce, of beets, potatoes, and carrots, and walked between the green pepper and tomato and string bean plants. He crossed the melon, strawberry, and cucumber patches, went around the raspberry and blackberry bushes, and walked under the apple, peach, plum, and pear trees in his fruit orchard.

Sassy quacked loudly as Mr. MacDonald closed the garden gate and hung his hoe on the side of the garage. He backed his little red truck from the garage and was on his way. Soon he was at the city dog pound. A young man was at the desk.

"I want a dog—a watch dog," Mr. MacDonald said. "He must have a loud bark so I'll know when people stop at my fruit and vegetable stand."

The young man smiled. "I have just the dog for you. Come with me."

They walked past pens of yipping puppies and barking dogs. The young man stopped beside a pen where a large brown and black German shepherd was sleeping.

"This is the dog," he said.

"But—but—he's sleeping! He isn't barking like the others. He doesn't look like a watch dog."

"He's used to the noise here. He only barks when there's a good reason. Alex! Wake up!"

The big dog jumped up. He looked at Mr. MacDonald and barked a deep, loud "Bow-wow-wow-wow!"

The young man smiled. "He's not cross, but he's noisy."

Mr. MacDonald held out his hand. "Come, Alex," he said. The dog put his nose against the screen and wagged his tail. Mr. MacDonald smiled. "I'll take him" he said.

When they were home he chained Alex in the shade beside the fruit and vegetable stand. He gave the dog a dish of water and a pan of dog food, which he'd bought on the way home. Sassy stood beside the stand, quacking and watching.

"Now Alex, be sure to bark when someone stops," Mr. MacDonald said, and went behind the house to his garden.

Alex gobbled up the dog food and stretched out for a nap. Pretty soon a car stopped. A woman got out and walked to the stand, looking toward the house. But Alex slept on. "I wonder where Mr. MacDonald is?" the woman said aloud.

Sassy waddled around the corner of the house. She stopped beside Alex. "Quack! Quack! Quack! Quack!" she called in Alex's ear.

The dog jumped up. He saw the car and the woman. "Bow-wow-wow-wow!" he barked.

Mr. MacDonald came running. "It worked!" he panted as he pushed his tattered straw hat back and wiped his bald head.

The woman bought tomatoes, green beans, potatoes, and apples. When she was gone Mr. MacDonald petted Alex. "Good dog," he said. Alex wagged his tail and Sassy quacked.

Many days later Mrs. Arnold, the next-door neighbor, told Mr. MacDonald that whenever she looked out, Alex was sleeping.

"How can that be?" Mr. MacDonald asked. "He always barks to tell me I have a customer."

"Yes, he barks," Mrs. Arnold said, "but not until Sassy quacks in his ear to wake him up."

"That lazy dog," Mr. MacDonald laughed. "But I like him, and as long as Sassy wakes him up and he barks to call me, everything will be fine."

Mr. MacDonald chuckled as he went back to his garden. "Those two are quite a team—quite a team," he said.

Discussion and Oral Exercises:

■ Content and comprehension questions such as the following can be asked:

Why did Mr. MacDonald want a dog?

What is a dog pound?

What did Mr. MacDonald mean when he said that Sassy and Alex were "quite a team?"

Name the vegetables and fruits that grew in Mr. MacDonald's garden.

■ Use the following question to stimulate interest in learning about bees:

Why did the bumblebee crawl inside the squash blossom? Continue with a discussion on the life and habits of bees. See an encyclopedia for further information on bumblebees and honeybees.

■ Vocabulary-in-context questions:

We heard, in the story, that Mr. MacDonald wore a "tattered straw hat." Does that mean he was wearing a brand new straw hat?

Sassy, the duck, waddled around the corner of the house. What does *waddle* mean? (Some children may enjoy demonstrating a duck waddling.)

Mr. MacDonald chuckled when he learned about the teamwork between Sassy and Alex. What does *chuckle* mean?

- Have the children retell the story. Emphasize speaking like the characters.
- Dramatize the story.

63. Changing Plans (1-3)

Listening Experience: Hearing and discussing a story about being calm when facing danger.

Charles Francis Hill screwed the lid on an empty pickle jar and called to his mother from the doorway of the long ranch house.

"I'm going to catch insects to take to school tomorrow. I'll bet I'll find more than anyone in my class!"

Mrs. Hill waved. "All right. Are you warm enough?"

Charles skipped past Duke, who was gnawing on a bone, and ran toward a clump of dry grass. "I'm too warm!" He threw his jacket open. "The sun is hot!" He kicked the grass and pounced on a fat brown cricket that hopped out. He put the insect into his glass jar and quickly screwed the cover on again.

"You're all right," he whispered to the cricket. "You'll get air through the holes in the lid."

Mrs. Hill called, "It's after four, so don't go far. It turns cold fast when the sun drops behind the mountains."

"O.K." Charles answered as he ran to an ant hill. Soon a large black ant was scurrying around the bottom of the jar.

Charles wandered up a trail toward the mountains. In the distance he could hear the bleating ba-a-a-a-a of the sheep his father raised on their ranch. He wondered if his pet lamb was with the flock. Maybe he wouldn't know Tiny, for she would have grown. He hadn't seen her since school started several weeks before.

"There sure aren't many insects around," he said aloud. He kicked a piece of old gray wood and a large brown ground beetle rushed to hide in the damp dirt. Charles dug him out and carefully lifted the jar lid and slid the beetle inside.

"I *guess* you're an insect," he said trying to count the beetle's squirming legs through the glass jar. "Anyway, you have six legs."

He looked up. "Oh! A butterfly! I've got to catch him!" He ran, following the zigzagging orange, brown, and black butterfly. But it kept just ahead of him—just far enough so that Charles was sure he'd catch him soon. So he didn't worry when he had left the trail. The butterfly settled down on some sagebrush. Charles crept up, his heart pounding. He reached out, but not fast enough, for again the butterfly was zigzagging up the mountain ahead of him.

Following the flitting butterfly from bush to bush was so exciting that Charles didn't think about getting tired. Up and up he went, around the boulders and rocks, this way and that. Again he was close to the butterfly. It was resting on a small bush on the edge of a steep cliff. Its wings were slowly moving up and down, up and down, up and down.

He crouched down and carefully reached out. His hand closed. He had it! He sat down, shook the cricket and ant down to the bottom of the jar with the beetle, and carefully put the butterfly inside. Four insects. He had hoped to get more. Maybe he'd find some others on the way back home.

Charles shivered. The sun had gone down and the air was cold. He'd be glad to get home and have a good supper. Somewhere nearby the sheep bleated and called to one another as they gathered together for the night.

Charles turned around slowly. "Which way?" he said aloud. He thought he had come from the left. He looked around. He shivered again. That high pointed rock over there—he didn't remember passing it. He turned slowly, his heart pounding. Nothing looked right. He was lost! He didn't know the way home and soon it would be dark!

It was so quiet! Insects always are still when the air is cold, but it was so very still. What was he going to do? If he had only brought Duke with him — Duke would have known the way home. Maybe the dog would hear if he called.

Setting the insect jar at his feet, Charles cupped his hands around his mouth and shouted, "Here, Duke! Here, Duke!" He called until his throat hurt, but there was no answering bark from his dog — only the sad, lonely bleating of the sheep as they settled down for the night.

Charles was scared. And he was cold. He put his hands into the pockets of his thin blue nylon jacket. He might as well keep walking. Maybe soon he'd see the lights of the ranch house. Charles strained his eyes against the soft twilight. Maybe it wasn't dark enough yet to see the lights.

He might have to spend the night alone in the mountains. He bit his lip. He wouldn't get panicky.

Suddenly he stopped walking. The sheep sounded nearer now. If he could find them he wouldn't be alone. Following the sound of the bleating flock, he turned to the right. He must hurry for soon it would be very dark. You could fall over a cliff in the dark. He stopped to listen. The sheep sounded very near.

Suddenly he had an awful thought. Suppose he frightened the sheep and the flock ran away from him! He must walk quietly.

Charles shivered. His feet were cold, too. An owl hooted. How lonely the owl sounded!

Where were the sheep? They had seemed so close, but now they were quiet. He would keep walking. He must find them.

Now it was pitch dark. All at once he stumbled. Trying to balance himself, he reached out his hand. They landed on something soft, something soft and warm. Wool! His fingers were deep in the warm oily wool of a sheep! He had found the flock!

Charles reached carefully to the right and touched a wet nose. They were all around him. Warm, woolly sheep. If he could stay close to them they would help to keep him warm. He sat down, surrounded by warm animals.

The cold night air was very still. The only sounds were the hoot of the owl and the breathing of the sheep. He napped, waking often to snuggle close to a woolly body. It seemed morning would never come. Surely someone would find him when it was daylight. His mother and father must be very worried.

His insect jar! Where was it? Then he remembered. He hadn't picked it up when he'd stopped to call Duke. He wouldn't have any insects to take to school. He swallowed hard. "You're all right," he told himself. He fell asleep again.

At last morning came. A crow cawed and scolded him from a nearby bush. "Caw! Caw! Caw!" The big black bird flew low to look at him.

The sheep were waking up. Some of them were picking a few blades of dry, frosty grass. They began sounding the soft ba-a-a-a call which Charles had long ago decided was their way of talking to one another. They looked at him, but they were not frightened. Walking slowly through the flock, he found Tiny, the lamb he had raised on the bottle. She was so big that now her name didn't suit her, but she recognized him. She seemed really glad to see him. He hugged her.

All at once the flock became quiet. They were listening. Straining his ears, he heard it long before he saw it overhead— the pounding, buzzing, slow-flying helicopter that belonged to a neighboring ranch owner.

Waving both arms wildly, he shouted, "Here I am! Here I am! See me? I'm right here!"

Frightened sheep ran in every direction as the helicopter slowly and noisily settled down a short distance below him. A moment later he was safe in his father's arms. His father's voice sounded strange as he said, "You're all right?"

"I'm hungry!" Charles said, yelling above the roar of the motor. "And I don't have any insects to take to school because I lost the jar!"

His father looked very tired. "No," he said, "but you can tell about spending the night in the mountains."

Charles laughed. "And about how the sheep kept me warm

—and the butterfly I followed and caught—and Dad, I was scared all right, but not too scared."

"You're a brave boy. I'm proud of you. Now, let's get to the helicopter, and get home to your mother."

His father lifted him into the helicopter.

"Hi, Mr. Welsh," Charles said to the pilot. "I'm sure glad you found me."

"So am I. Fasten your belt and we'll be off."

"O.K. And I'll tell the kids about my helicopter ride and—and—boy! Am I ever hungry!"

The helicopter lifted from the ground and swung down the mountain toward the ranch.

Discussion and Oral Exercises:

■ Ask comprehension questions such as the following:
   The title of this story is "Changing Plans." What plans changed?
   How do you think Charles felt when he was lost?
   Why was it good that he kept calm?

■ Have you ever been lost? (Lead into a discussion of the need to keep calm in times of danger; if separated from parents, the advantage of knowing your home address and telephone number.)

■ Have children retell the story. Later they may dramatize it.

Correlate with: Lesson 48, "Butterflies"
                    Lesson 50, "Hopping with Harvey"
                    Lesson 70, "Emergency"
                    Lesson 75, "Now What?"

64. How Well Did You Listen? (2-3)

Listening Experience: Paying attention to a short informative report and discussing it from memory.

Bombo is a two-year-old chimpanzee who lives with Mr. and Mrs. Donald Hall and their two children, Susan and Dick.

Perhaps Bombo thinks he is a child, too. He wears Dick's outgrown clothing. He sits in Susan's old high chair to eat his meals and he sleeps in her baby crib. He plays games with the brother and sister. He pulls up a chair to reach the cookie jar. He acts very much like a small child.

Bombo is quite intelligent, but there is one important thing which children do easily that Bombo is unable to do. He can't talk.

Chimpanzees understand many of the things that humans say but they cannot talk, because the muscles, or vocal cords, in their throats are different from those of humans.

Discussion and Oral Exercises:

■ Ask comprehension questions such as the following:
  How old is Bombo?
  What does *intelligent* mean?
  Mention some things that Bombo does that show he is intelligent.
  Why can't chimpanzees talk?

Variation:

■ Use brief paragraphs of informative material from various subject matter areas (science, social studies) and orally test the children for listening skills.

65. Let's Pretend (2-3)

Listening Experience: Hearing about, imagining, and discussing experiences of the senses — sight, hearing, smell, taste, touch.

Karen and John were home from school with colds. They couldn't go outside and they were tired of television, records, and games.

Karen said, "We could play 'Let's Pretend.'"

"How?" John asked.

"Well—let's pretend it's recess at school and we're on the playground. What would we see and hear?"

John jumped up. "I'd see Jimmy and Bruce hanging by their feet from the monkey bar, and you'd be on the swings."

Karen laughed. "And the swing would squea-ea-ea-k, and my feet would scuff against the dirt as I tried to go higher—."

John interrupted, "And a jet is going over. It sounds like faraway thunder. It's going fast! There's a white streak behind it all across the blue sky."

"That's a vapor trail!"

"O.K. There's a vapor trail that's like a straight line close to the jet, but way back behind the plane the vapor trail is kind of fuzzy, like it's breaking up."

"It's disappearing into the air," Karen said.

John went on, "And the big boys are on the ball field—"

"They're yelling," Karen continued. "Tom Gordon is arguing with Brian Luce. The other boys are standing around watching. Now more of them are yelling. Tom says Brian was out. They're about ready to fight!"

John exclaimed, "Oh! Brian hit Tom! Now the other boys are pulling them apart! I wonder why Brian fights so much?"

Karen shook her head. "I don't know. I guess he's a poor loser."

The children were quiet a moment, then John said, "Let's go on with our pretend game. It's fun."

Karen said, "I hear a robin singing in the apple tree beside the playground. The apple tree is in blossom; um-m-m-m, I can smell the apple blossoms. And Mrs. Robin is making her nest up there on a branch. She's using mud and string and dry grass."

John laughed. "How can you see the apple tree from the swing? It's on the other side of the school!"

"Well—I left the swing."

"You didn't say so. I'm going down the slide. Oh-o-oh! It's hot! Whoosh! Bang! Oh! My shoes are full of sand! They feel tight!"

"Hurry and empty out your shoes because the bell is ringing. As soon as you get your shoes on I'll race you to the door!"

John puffed. "You didn't beat! It was a tie!"

Karen got up. "The game's over. It was fun to have recess sitting at home in the living room."

Discussion and Oral Exercises:

- Pretend you're at the supermarket. What would you see? Hear? Smell? (Choose a child to start, and suggest that children add to the story as they have an idea.)
- Pretend we're having a picnic. What would we do? See? Smell? Taste?
- Pretend you're having dinner with your family. What would you hear? See? Smell? Taste? Touch?
- Pretend you've gone to the doctor. Tell what you might see, hear, smell, taste. Maybe you'd get a vaccination. How would it feel?
- Pretend you're in a dentist's office for your dental checkup. Tell what you would see as the dentist cleaned your teeth. How would it feel? What would you hear? Are there any unusual smells?

66. The New Coat (2-3)

Listening Experience: Hearing a story and empathizing with some of the characters.

Melba Berger had a new red coat. She had always wanted a

red coat, so she was proud and happy the first day she wore it to school. She would be very careful of it, because it had to last for two winters.

Sally Jones was also wearing a red coat when she got on the school bus that morning. Jack Anderson, a fifth-grade boy, shouted, "Two red coats! Watch out, fellows! The redcoats are coming!" Then Bruce Miller began to yell, "The redcoats are coming!"

Pretty soon five or six of the boys and girls were laughing about the red coats. Melba and Sally sat quietly with their eyes down. Would that bus ride never end?

As they were waiting for the school doors to open, Melba and Sally heard Pamela Wall say, "I don't like red because there are so many colors you can't wear with it. If you wear green, you look like a Christmas tree, and yellow or pink don't go well with it either."

"That's right," Penny Daly said. "I can't wear it because I'm blonde. Red doesn't do anything for a blonde, my mother says."

Sally took off her pink wool knit hat and stuffed it in her coat pocket. Melba pulled her coat together over her bright green dress and pushed her blonde hair under her scarf. She no longer felt happy.

How would you have felt?

Discussion and Oral Exercises:

■ Who were the redcoats the fifth-grade boy mentioned? (The teacher likely will need to explain briefly.)
■ Can you remember a time when your feelings were hurt? Do you care to tell us about it?
■ Sometimes we hurt a friend's feelings without meaning to. Can you remember ever saying something that you later wished you hadn't said? Would you like to tell us about it?

Correlate with: Lesson 30, "Guess Who"
                    Lesson 67, "The New School"

67. The New School (2-3)

Listening Experience: Hearing a story and empathizing
with the main character.

Sidney Bean had moved with his family to another part of
the city. On his first morning at the new school Miss Anderson
introduced him to the class. She said, "We have a new third-
grade boy with us. Boys and girls, this is Sidney Bean."

Sidney heard snickers and felt uncomfortable. He didn t
know why the children were laughing at him.

When they went out for morning recess one of the boys
from the room jumped up and down in front of Sidney and
sang, "Kidney Bean is tall and lean! Kidney Bean is tall and
lean!"

Sidney had always liked being tall. In the old school he was
proud that he was the tallest boy in the room. But these children were laughing at him.

Boys and girls from other rooms came to see what was happening. They were all looking at him and some were laughing.
Sidney didn't know what to do. He backed against the brick
wall of the school and stared at the ground.

A boy shouted, "I wonder what other Beans are in his
family?" He pushed Sidney. "Hey, Kidney! Do you have a
sister Lima?" Many of the children laughed.

A girl called, "How about Navy Bean?"

When the laughter died down the first boy yelled, "Kidney!
Do you have a brother Wax Bean—or String Bean?"

At last the bell rang. Sidney's face was red as he lined up
at the door. As he went inside he heard one boy remark, "Hey!
I've got it! He didn't get mad, so he's a Jelly Bean!"

How do you think Sidney felt?

Discussion and Oral Exercises:

■ Stimulate discussion with some or all of the following
questions:

The New School

Telling Tales

Why did the boys and girls tease Sidney? Why do people tease others? What would you have done in Sidney's place?

Do you think the boys and girls knew how Sidney felt? Why are children hurt when others make fun of their names?

A new boy or girl coming to a classroom usually feels strange and uncomfortable. What might the children have done to make Sidney's first day a happy one?

■ Discuss with the children the fact that most names have meanings, or had at some time. Perhaps the school or local library will have a book on the subject. Children would enjoy knowing the meaning of their names. Examples: *Johnson, Peterson (sen), Olson* are examples of "son of _____" names. *Taylor, Hunter, Fisher, Weaver,* are occupational names. German equivalents of these names are: *Schneider, Jaeger, Fischer,* and *Weber.*

Correlate with: Lesson 30, "Guess Who"
Lesson 66, "The New Coat"

68.   *Telling Tales (2-3)*

Listening Experience: Hearing a portion of a narrative and offering a plausible continuation.

In advance of the activity, prepare a spool or ball of string, mixing pieces of various lengths from 5 to 15 feet. Do not tie the pieces together at their ends.

The story tellers sit in a circle. The teacher or a volunteer from the group begins an original story as she unwinds the string. The story might be something like this:

Tom and Jeff are friends. One Saturday they took their

lunch and started on a hike. They took a bus to the end of the line, where there was a park with a little creek. They stopped to play by the creek near an old house. They made a dam of sticks and branches.

After a time they sat down to eat their lunch. As they were eating they heard a low, whimpering sound. They ran up the bank toward the old house. The sound grew louder . . . .

The storyteller has come to the end of the piece of string. She passes the ball to the child on her left, who adds to the story, making it up as he goes on slowly unwinding the next piece of string.

The story continues until everyone has had a turn or until a satisfactory ending is reached.

Variation:

■ To use this activity without a ball of string, prepare several two- or three-sentence beginnings which will serve as a starting point for the children. Example: "One day I went to the park. Beside the pond I met a boy who was crying."

When you have told your story beginning, choose a child to continue for a few sentences. The child in turn will select another to go on with the story. The storytelling continues until a satisfactory ending is reached.

Correlate with: Lesson 39, "Go On."

69. The Rescue (2-3)

Listening Experience: Hearing a long story and discussing ethical and civic issues raised in it.

Chang was scared. For the first time in the nine months of his Siamese cat life he was so scared he couldn't move. When he looked down from the fork of the tall elm tree his stomach flip-flopped and his heart pounded. He didn't know how to get down!

"Meow!" he wailed. "Me-o-o-o-w!" How he wished he had stayed in the house! But the door had been open; he had scooted outside before he'd known what he was doing, and right there before him was a lovely tall tree just right for a cat to climb.

Going up had been fun. His sharp claws dug into the rough elm bark and his strong claws pulled him along. But he'd stopped to look down, and now, here he was. "Me-o-o-ow! Meo-oow!" he cried, wedging himself tightly into the fork between the two branches.

Mrs. Brown, on her way to the post office, stopped and looked up. "Here, Kitty, Kitty, Kitty," she called.

"Me-o-ow! Me-o-o-o-ow!" Chang answered, pressing his stomach tightly against the tree.

"You'll come down when you're ready," Mrs. Brown said, and she went on.

Two boys coming home from school for lunch stopped to look up. "The cat's scared to come down," one of them said.

"Our cat stayed up in a tree overnight once when he was a kitten," the other one answered. "But he finally came down the next day." The boys went on.

More children came by, stopped to look up and call, then after a minute, went on.

At last Chang saw his own Matt and Kim coming. "Meo-o-ow! Meo-o-o-ow! Meo-o-o-o-ow!" he howled.

Kim screamed, "It's Chang! He'll fall! Matt, call Mom!"

Matt dashed into the house. "Mom!" he shouted. "Chang's in the elm tree and he can't get down!"

Mrs. Harlan ran to the front window. "How did he get outside?" she said. "Just a little while ago he was playing in the basement. He must have sneaked out when I went into the yard."

Kim, at the foot of the tree, reached up and called, "Here Chang, here Chang, here Chang. Come on down." But the cat only wailed.

"You might as well come in and eat lunch," Mrs. Harlan said. "He'll probably be down by the time you're finished."

But Chang wasn't down after lunch, nor was he down when the children hurried back from school in the afternoon.

"What are we going to do?" Kim asked, her eyes filled with tears.

"Maybe if we put cat food on the ground, he'll come down," Matt said, running to the house.

He returned with the cat food, and together the brother and sister coaxed and waited and coaxed, but Chang only clung fearfully to the fork in the tree and kept up his mournful cry for help.

"Daddy will be home soon. Maybe he can reach him with the long ladder," Matt said hopefully.

But when Mr. Harlan came home and looked up at the cat in the tree, he shook his head. "The ladder isn't long enough," he said. "That rascal must be thirty-five feet from the ground."

"Oh, no!" Kim cried.

"Maybe it will reach," Matt said hopefully. "Won't you try?"

"Please, Daddy, please," Kim begged.

"I don't think there's any use," their father said, "but after dinner we'll try. Anyway, he may be down by then."

By seven o'clock that evening the yard was full of neighbors. Several men went home to find out if their ladders were longer than Mr. Harlan's. It was no use. No one had a ladder long enough to reach Chang. People said again and again, "He'll come down when he's hungry enough." At last they all went home.

Mr. Harlan looked thoughtfully at the tall elm. "Any other tree in the neighborhood we could climb, but Chang chose the one that goes straight up for thirty-five feet before there are branches."

Kim burst into tears. "We can't leave him out here all night! He'll be cold and scared, and it might rain!"

Matt wiped his eyes on his shirt sleeve.

Mrs. Harlan gave each child a kiss. "Don't worry, darlings.

It's not very cold tonight, and see—there's almost a full moon. It won't rain. He'll be all right."

Kim blew her nose. "But he might go to sleep and fall!"

"He won't fall," her father said.

Several times that night the children awoke and ran out on the porch to see how the cat was doing. Watching from the fork of the tree, Chang cried his lonely cry when he saw them.

In the morning they sadly waved goodby to their pet and went to school. "I'm worried. He must be starving," Kim said. "He hasn't had anything to eat since yesterday morning."

At lunch time the children stopped at the tree only a minute before they rushed inside.

"Mama!" Kim cried. "Mr. Freeman says maybe the firemen can get Chang down! They have long ladders!"

"Your teacher has a good idea," Mrs. Harlan said. "While you're eating lunch, I'll call the fire department."

The children could hear their mother explaining what had happened. There was a long wait, then she said quietly, "I see," and hung up the receiver.

"What did they say?" both children asked at once.

"The man said if they start rescuing cats from trees they won't be ready for the fire calls. He suggested we try the Humane Society."

"Will you try right now, Mom, before we go back to school?" Matt asked.

"Yes, right away." Mrs. Harlan looked up the number and dialed. Again she explained Chang's predicament and asked if someone could come to rescue him.

It seemed like a long time before she again said, "I see." She listened again and said, "We've tried that. Thanks anyway."

"They won't come either?" Kim asked fearfully.

"No. They don't have insurance on their men to climb trees. The woman said they can't risk the safety of a man for a cat. She thinks Chang will come down when he's hungry enough."

"But he's too afraid!" Kim cried.

"What are we going to do?" Matt worried.

"The woman at the Humane Society suggested that we try the Parks Department. They have long ladders that they use when they trim trees."

Kim jumped up and down. "Oh, yes! We saw them working in the park near the school, didn't we, Matt?"

"Hurry, Mom! Call right now!" Matt urged.

Again they waited and waited while their mother listened patiently to the voice at the other end. Finally she said, "Thank you. I understand." She slowly hung the receiver up.

"They won't come either," Matt said flatly.

"No. The man was very nice, but he said it would be too expensive to send a crew and a truck out here, and that the public wouldn't want the city to make a practice of spending time and money in rescuing cats."

Kim was crying softly. "It's been so long. He'll starve up there."

"We'll think of something," her mother said. "Hurry now, or you'll be late for school."

"I can't do any work," Kim complained.

"Let us stay home," Matt begged. "All we can think about is Chang up there in the tree. Please, Mom."

"No. We're doing everything we can. And you never can tell—he just might decide to come down by himself. Run along now."

At three-thirty Matt came running home five minutes ahead of Kim. Pausing just long enough to call, "Hi, Chang!" he was inside the kitchen door before the cat finished his sad answering wail.

"Mom!" he called. "I think we can get Chang down! I told the kids about Chang, and Jim Stein says his father can get him down!"

"He'll need a very long ladder. Is he a painter?" Mrs. Harlan asked.

"No." He gave his mother a scrap of paper. "Here's the phone number. Jim says if we'll call, he's sure his dad will come over and get Chang down. Call right away, will you?"

"Take it easy, Matt," Mrs. Harlan said. "How can this man get Chang down?"

"He has climbers—the things he puts on his feet to climb telephone poles."

"He works for the telephone company?"

"Yes. But hurry, Mom! Call the number!"

Mrs. Harlan was talking to Mrs. Stein when Kim came in. Matt told his sister what was happening.

When she hung up, Mrs. Harlan was smiling. "Mrs. Stein says her husband will be home from work around five o'clock and she's sure he'll be able to rescue Chang."

"Goody! Let's go tell Chang!" Kim cried.

High up in the fork of the tree, hungry, tired and thirsty, Chang mewed a faint welcome.

"You'll be down soon," Kim called.

"Just a little while longer," Matt added.

The neighborhood children gathered in the Harlan yard, all eager to see what would happen. When a red car pulled into the drive they rushed to meet Mr. Stein and Jim.

"This is very nice of you, Mr. Stein," Mrs. Harlan said.

"Glad to do it," Mr. Stein answered, looking up at Chang. He put on the metal climbing spikes and snapped his strong belt around the tree. Then he started the climb, driving one sharp spike and then the other into the tree as he went up, step after step. It didn't take long before his face was level with the cat.

Holding firmly to the branch, Mr. Stein petted the cat for a minute. "Want to go down, boy?" he asked.

"Meow-ow-ow-ow," Chang said as he licked Mr. Stein's hand.

"Come on, then." As he lifted the cat, Chang clawed the air wildly.

"You're all right," the man said. "I won't let you fall."

Still firmly holding to the branch with his left hand, he pushed Chang inside his partly zipped jacket and pulled the zipper to the top.

The watchers below were quiet as Mr. Stein climbed slowly down, one step after the other. When he was on the ground at last, a big cheer went up from the children.

Mr. Stein opened his jacket and Chang peeped out cautiously. Then, seeing that he was down, he leaped to the ground and dashed to the dish of food that had been waiting for him. Mrs. Harlan brought him a pan of water. He lapped thirstily and then rushed back to the cat food. Everyone stood around him in a circle, smiling and talking.

Matt said, "Thank you, Mr. Stein."

"Thank you so very much," Kim added.

And, that night, Chang and the children once again slept soundly.

Discussion and Oral Exercises:

■ What kind of cat was Chang? (If the children are not familiar with the breed, describe a Siamese cat.) How long was Chang in the tree?

■ The following questions are related to government and community services. If the class is a mature one, the discussion may lead to a discussion of government services on a county, state, and national level.

Why did the fire department refuse to help?

Why did the Humane Society refuse to help? What does the Humane Society do?

The man from the Parks Department said, "The public wouldn't want the city to spend time and money rescuing cats." What, or who, is the public? Why would the public be concerned?

What are taxes?

Besides the fire and parks departments, do you know any other public services that are paid for with tax money? (police, street cleaning, schools, health department, post office, and the like.)

■ Have the children retell the story. Each child might talk for one minute.

■ Have the children dramatize the part of the story they liked best.

Correlate with: Lesson 16, "Stealing the Cat's Mouse"

70. *Emergency (2-3)*

Listening Experience: Hearing about and understanding the development of an emergency, then trying to solve the problem.

The telephone rang and Bruce ran to answer. "Yes, this is Bruce." He listened and then said, "Just a minute. I'll ask my mother."

"Mom," he called, "Mike wants to know if I can come over."

Mrs. Fujita put the baby in her crib. "If you know the way," she agreed.

"I can find it easy!"

"Just a minute, Bruce! We haven't been in this neighborhood long enough for you to know these streets. Tell me how you get to Mike's"

"Mom! You drove me back from there the other night! Don't you remember?" Bruce zipped his jacket.

"I remember, but do you?" Mrs. Fujita asked.

"Of course! I'm old enough!"

"Tell me," his mother said quietly.

"You go up to the corner where the green house is, and then you turn right and go as far as the bus stop, and then you turn right again for a couple more blocks — I think."

"That's not it exactly. Now listen. When you get to the bus stop, turn left."

"All right. I'll find it. I know the house."

"Be home by 5:30," his mother called as he went out.

He started walking. After living in the neighborhood only two weeks, he wondered how people knew their own homes. So many of the houses looked alike. And the streets had strange names like Ridgeway, Cambridge, and Rocky Hollow. Now, what was Mike's street called? He couldn't remember, but it didn't matter. He'd know the house because Mike's tent was beside the garage.

Before long Bruce knew something was wrong. The bus stop wasn't where he thought it should have been. He turned right, then left, then right again. Because he didn't know the name of Mike's street, he couldn't ask anyone for directions. He decided he might as well go home.

He turned around. If he found Sleepy Hollow, his own street, he'd be all right. He walked and walked, looking at street signs and turning one corner after another. That house on his left with the trees in front—he'd passed it before this afternoon. Only—it was on the other side of the street then. No. He had his directions all mixed up. He didn't know which way to go.

Suddenly Bruce had an idea. What do you think he did?

Discussion and Oral Exercises:

■ As the children mention them, discuss various ways of solving the problem. Some possible solutions are:
   a) Stop someone on the street and ask directions for Sleepy Hollow Street.
   b) Knock on a door and ask if you can use the telephone to call home.
   c) Go to the nearest store, if there is one, and ask direc tions there.
■ Why did Bruce have trouble finding Mike's house? Do you think he listened when his mother gave him directions?
■ Stress the importance of knowing your own home address and telephone number. Teach directions by putting cards labeled *North, South, East,* and *West* on the proper sides of the classroom. Demonstrate that compass directions are more reliable than *left, right.* Would it have been easier for Bruce if he and his mother had used compass directions in

talking about the way to Mike's house? Throughout the discussion, stress the need to keep calm in anxiety-causing situations.

Correlate with: Lesson 13, "Bus Station"
                      Lesson 18, "Follow My Directions"
                      Lesson 63, "Changing Plans"
                      Lesson 75, "Now What?"

71. The Largest Animal in the World (2-3)

Listening Experience: Hearing a story related to a familiar experience and discussing its informational content.

Dennis's mother and father came into the living room. They looked so nice in their party clothes.

"If you and Linda get hungry, Dennis, there are cookies in the cookie jar and there's chocolate milk in the refrigerator," his mother said as she pulled on her gloves. "Be a good boy, and go to bed when Linda says it's time, won't you?"

"I will. I wish she'd come. I hope she has a new riddle story tonight." The bell rang. "Here she is!" He opened the door.

"Hi, Linda! Did you think of another riddle story?"

"Take it easy, Dennis," his father said with a smile. "Give Linda time to get her breath."

"I don't mind, Mr. Arnold. Telling stories is good practice for me. I'm going to be a teacher when I finish school."

"I'm sure you'll be a good one," Mr. Arnold said.

Dennis kissed his parents goodnight and waved as they left in the car.

Linda sat down on the floor. "How would you like a riddle story about a giant?" she asked.

"That sounds good. Is he a big huge giant?"

"Very, very huge. The hugest giant in the world. Only this is a female giant, and she has a baby that's bigger than an elephant."

Dennis laughed. "You can't fool me this time. It's a fairy story. There aren't any giants now."

Linda nodded her head. "Oh yes, there are," she said. "Just wait. This giant and her big baby live in the water."

"Now I know it's not true! People can't live in the water!"

"This giant is not a person, but she's an animal. She is the biggest animal in the world. Can you guess now?"

Dennis thought a minute. "She might be a hippopotamus; they're pretty big. No, I saw a hippo at the zoo and he wasn't as big as an elephant. I give up. Tell me."

"This giant animal is a whale."

"Is a whale a fish?" Dennis asked.

"No. Whales' bodies are streamlined and shaped like a fish body, and they do live in the water. But a whale is not a fish; it's a mammal. People are mammals. So are horses and dogs and monkeys."

"But mammals breathe air," Dennis argued. "They drown in water."

"Our mother whale would drown if she couldn't come up for air," Linda explained. "She can stay under the water much longer than people can. Whales can stay under for half an hour, or even longer if they are frightened. But then they must come up and get fresh air. They blow the stale air out of their lungs through holes in the tops of their heads. Then they take a deep breath of fresh air and dive into the ocean again. Whales breathe through these holes in the top of their heads just as people breathe through their noses."

"I'd like to see a whale," Dennis said. "Is there one at the zoo?"

"No. Whales live in the ocean, which is salt water. Most zoos don't have either the salt water or a tank large enough for a whale to live in," Linda explained.

"Tell me about the whale baby," Dennis said. "What does it eat?"

"Baby whales drink milk."

"Linda! Where can they get milk in the ocean?"

"I know it seems strange, Dennis, but whale babies are born alive just like kittens or puppies. The mother whale nurses its baby just like other mammals do. After the baby whale is about a year old it eats tiny shrimp and other small sea animals. The mother whale loves her baby and tries to protect him from enemies."

"Will the mother whale hurt people?" Dennis asked.

"She's a friendly animal. She wouldn't attack a boat unless she was wounded. There are many kinds of whales. The mother whale I'm talking about is a great blue whale, which is the largest kind. Blue whales are especially friendly. They like company and travel in groups. They never fight among themselves, but often play together, chasing each other and splashing around. Sometimes, big as they are, they leap right out of the water."

Dennis thought a minute. "If a whale baby is bigger than an elephant, how big is the mother whale?"

"The mother blue whale weighs as much as twenty-five elephants, and is about one hundred feet long."

"Man! Twenty-five elephants! Now I see why they don't have one at the zoo! That was a good riddle story, Linda. Wait till I tell my friend Eddie that there really are giant animals in the world today."

Dennis started toward the kitchen. "I'm hungry. Let's have some cookies and milk."

Discussion and Oral Exercises:

■ To stimulate further discussion about whales, begin with questions such as these:

What kind of whale was the mother whale in the story? Is that a friendly whale?

The mother whale was as heavy as how many elephants?
The baby whale was as heavy as how many elephants?

Where do you suppose Linda learned so much about whales?

■ The following questions are based on the information in the story, but a few go beyond the story. The answers may be brought out in discussion, or you may wish to have some pupils consult a children's encyclopedia for more information about whales. For your information, see the very extensive discussion in the *Britannica.*

How do whales differ from fish?

If whales are animals that breathe air, why don't they live on land?

Can you think of some reasons? Could a whale drown?

Why don't we see whales in most zoos?

What do big whales eat? What food do baby whales have when they are very young?

■ The following questions extend the discussion:

How many mammals do you suppose we can think of? (Have each child name one, continuing around the room as many times as children can name mammals.)

Think about the things that all animals, including fish, mammals, birds, insects, etc., need to live. (air, food, water, and the like)

What can we say that's true about all animals? (Some examples: they need air in some form; they can move about; their food is plants or other animals; they need water.)

72. *The Transparent Chinese Dragon Fighting Fish (2-3)*

Listening Experiences: Hearing a humorous story.
Discussing how people feel when they have been fooled.

Mr. Miller was discouraged. His pet shop business was not doing well. He had puppies, hamsters, goldfish, birds, and monkeys, but nobody came to buy them.

"If I can only find a way to get people into my shop," he thought. "If they came in, they might buy."

Suddenly Mr. Miller smiled. Then he laughed right out loud. When he laughed the monkeys chattered, the dogs barked, and the parrot squawked.

"It's worth trying," he said to the animals as he went into the back room. There he made a cardboard sign that said in big black letters, TRANSPARENT CHINESE DRAGON FIGHTING FISH. He filled a fish bowl with water and placed the sign beside the bowl in the shop window.

In a couple of minutes a man stopped, read the sign, and stared at the bowl. A woman stopped. Two boys on their way home from school moved in to look. Within a few minutes a crowd of people had gathered outside the pet shop window. Those in the back were standing on tiptoe to get a better look at the transparent Chinese dragon fighting fish.

"Look!" exclaimed a man, "they're fighting! See the ripples in the water?"

"That's right!" a woman said. "They really are fighting!"

A woman at the back called, "Make room for others! We want to see too!" She crowded her way to the front, pushing other people out of her way.

"I'm going to get a pair of those fish! I've never seen anything like them!" the first man said as he hurried into the shop. A dozen others followed him.

Mr. Miller came toward the first man. "Can I help you?" he asked, smiling happily.

"I want a pair of those transparent fighting fish," the man said.

Mr. Miller's pleasant smile disappeared. He scratched his bald head and stared down at the red plaid shirt over his round stomach.

"Well—" he began slowly.

"How much are they?" someone called.

"I was first!" the man exclaimed. "If you have only one pair, I should have them."

Mr. Miller looked very sad. "Well, you see, it's like this. I have only one pair and they're not for sale."

A roar went up from the crowd. "Not for sale!" the first man exclaimed in an angry voice. "Then why are they in the window?"

"They're very hard to get, and they're expensive. I—I wanted people to see them I guess."

"How much are they? Rare fish always are expensive," a woman commented.

"They're—they're fifteen dollars a pair. And, as you'd expect, they're hard to care for. They sometimes eat one another. They get sick easily too. You're not even sure when one has died, since they're transparent."

"Would you take orders?" a man with a briefcase asked.

"No. I don't know how long it would be before I could get more," Mr. Miller answered. "But if you're looking for fish, I have many kinds that are more interesting to watch than the Chinese dragon. You can see them and they aren't as expensive." Mr. Miller motioned toward his well kept aquariums. But no one was interested in fish you could see.

Several people were standing near the window, staring into the fish bowl.

"There, see that! They're having a battle! Look at those ripples!" the first man exclaimed. More people crowded in to look.

One of the schoolboys laughed. "There aren't any fish in there! The water ripples when a truck goes past because it shakes the building!"

The people became very quiet. Everyone looked at Mr. Miller. He laughed uncomfortably. Finally he said, "The boy is right. There are no transparent fish. It was meant as a joke. I thought people would notice the sign and have a good laugh. I thought maybe they'd come in to talk, and maybe while they were here they would see a pet they wanted—one they could look at."

No one laughed. Some people left without a word. The ones who had seen the ripples were angry.

"You'll never see me in here again!" the first man shouted. He slammed the door behind him.

"You'll find it doesn't pay to play pranks on the public," a woman said.

"Dishonesty never pays," another woman muttered.

"No one likes to be made to look foolish," a young woman said to her husband as they turned to go.

Soon all the people were gone. Not one had bought anything. Mr. Miller took the sign from the window. He shook his head. "My plan backfired," he said. "If I live to be a hundred, I'll never understand the public."

Discussion and Oral Exercises:

■ Begin with a few comprehension questions to stimulate discussion:

What does *transparent* mean?

Why were the people angry? Do you think they should have been angry?

■ Have you ever played a trick on someone? Did the person think it was funny? Do you like to have tricks played on you? Why?

■ Have children retell the story.

■ Have children dramatize the story.

73. Let's Talk This Over (2-3)

Listening Experience: Hearing stories about problems in interpersonal relations and discussing possible solutions.

Present a fictitious anecdote about a problem situation common to most groups of young children. Avoid using names of children in the class. Here is an example; another one follows.

Problem 1.

It was time for morning recess, and children were going to the hall to get their jackets and coats. Pam and Tom were ahead of Ronald, who always wanted to be first.

"Let me get my coat!" Ronald said, pushing Tom against Pam. She fell, hurting her knee.

Seizing his coat, Ronald dashed back to the room.

"I'm going to tell!" Pam said, as she got up and started toward Miss Howard's desk.

Tom zipped his jacket. "I don't like Ronald," he muttered, following Pam to the teacher's desk.

Miss Howard listened to the children. Then she said, "After recess we'll talk together about the problem of being first. As all of you know, we have had this problem before, and we need to work it out together."

Discussion and Oral Exercises:

■ Children should be encouraged to express their honest feelings about this situation and to bring up topics which they feel might contribute to solving the problem. The following questions cover only a few of many aspects of this situation that may lend themselves to group discussion and problem solving.

Why do some people think it's so important to be first? Do you think that it is?

Do you think it's unfair to the others if one child is always first?

What are your feelings toward someone who insists on being first all the time?

■ Propose solutions for the children to discuss. Here are three possibilities:

What would happen if one child were to be first in all activities during one school day, then another on the next day, and so on until every child had a day of being first, and then we would start over?

What if each child tried to consider whether it is really important to be first before making an issue of a situation?

If some children continue to have difficulty about being
first, could they sit down together to try to work out
their problems themselves, without getting the whole
class into the discussion?

Problem 2.
Many children in Mrs. Garcia's room liked the coat hook
nearest the door. Leo took Hal's coat off the hook and put it on
another; then he hung his jacket on the first hook.

Hal rushed to Mrs. Garcia's desk. "Leo moved my coat and
took the first hook!" he complained.

"I did not!" Leo shouted.

"I saw you!"

Mrs. Garcia said, "Since I didn't see what happened, I
don't know which of you is right. Only Leo and Hal know. Why
don't you boys talk it over and see if you can work the problem
out by yourselves?"

The boys went into the hall, where they talked for several
minutes. Then Leo took his coat down and hung Hal's on the
first hook near the door.

Discussion and Oral Exercises:
■ How do you think they solved the problem? What might
Leo have said? What might Hal have said?
■ Role playing of the incident, after discussion, is effective.

74. *The Invisible Birthday Present (2-3)*

Listening Experience: Through listening, becoming aware
of the rewards of being helpful
and thoughtful within the family.

Tony opened his eyes. It was late, for the sun was high in
the sky. Suddenly he remembered! Today was his mother's

birthday and he didn't have a present for her. But what was even worse, he couldn't buy a present because he didn't have any money.

Tony got out of bed and went to the window. Three stories below, trucks and cars rumbled and bumped over the broken place in the pavement, but he hardly saw them. He might as well tell his mother right away that he didn't have a present for her.

He dressed, dropping his pajamas beside the bed on top of yesterday's dirty clothes. His room was a mess, with toys and clothes scattered over the floor. Tossing back his dark curly hair, he started toward the kitchen. The apartment was very quiet.

"Mama!" he called. He looked around. There was a note on the kitchen table.

> Tony, bambino,
>
> I've been called to work at the Pizza Palace today. Mrs. DeLucca said she will give you lunch. I'll be home by 6 tonight.
>
> Mama

After a breakfast of cold cereal and milk, Tony put his dishes in the nearly full sink. Last night the apartment had been so hot that his mother hadn't washed the supper dishes. Instead, they had sat on the back porch until bedtime.

Tony wished his father wasn't so far away, working on a bridge construction job. His father would have given him money to buy his mother a present, but he wouldn't be home for two weeks. Suddenly Tony began to smile. Then he laughed right out loud. He ran hot water in the sink and washed and dried the dishes. He cleaned the gas range. He swept the floor and then wiped it with a sponge mop. He carried the papers and garbage outside.

In his bedroom Tony put his toys on the shelf and stuffed the diry clothes into the clothes hamper. He hung his pajamas in the closet and made his bed. Then he got out the vacuum cleaner and went over the rugs in the living room and the bedrooms. He dusted all of the tables, chairs, and window sills. As he worked Tony whistled, "Happy Birthday to You."

When he was finished he took a clean piece of white paper and his crayons. He smiled to himself as he folded the paper into a birthday card and drew flowers on the outside. On the inside he wrote:

Dear Mama,

    I am going to give you an in . . .

He stopped writing and thought. Finally he opened the front door of the apartment and poked his head out into the hall.

"Mrs. DeLucca!" he shouted.

"Yes, Tony," a voice came from the apartment across the hall.

"How do you spell *invisible*?"

"I-n-v-i-s-i-b-l-e," the neighbor called back. "Lunch is almost ready, Tony."

"O.K. I'll be over in a minute." Tony finished writing on the card.

Later that afternoon he set the table and put the birthday card at his mother's place. When he heard his mother coming up the stairs, he ran to meet her.

"Hi, Mama!" he shouted. Then he sang, "Happy birthday to you! Happy birthday to you! Happy birthday, dear Mama, Happy birthday to you!"

His mother laughed and then kissed him. "Thank you, Tony. I didn't know you'd remember it was my birthday."

"I did! And guess what? I have a new kind of birthday present for you!"

"You have? I can't wait to see it!"

Tony giggled as they went into the kitchen. His mother looked around. "Where is it?" she asked.

Tony was jumping up and down with excitement "You can't see it! See if you can guess!"

His mother saw the card. She picked it up. "Thank you, darling, for making me a card. You know I like flowers, don't you?" She looked inside. "You are giving me an invisible present. No one ever gave me an invisible present before. What can it be?'

"Guess!" Tony shouted. "See if you can guess!"

She looked around the kitchen. "You washed the dishes and you washed the floor. You carried out the garbage."

"There's more," Tony said. They went to the living room "And you cleaned this room, too!"

"That's part of the present, but there's more!" Tony pulled his mother toward the bedrooms.

She looked pleased. "Tony, you've done a wonderful job of cleaning the apartment! I was dreading having to do it to-night. Thank you!" She gave him another hug and a kiss. "You've given me a very nice birthday surprise. But it's not invisible. Everything you've done shows—I can see it."

Tony laughed. "That's only part of it. The things I'm going to help you with tomorrow and the next day and the next, you can't see. I'm going to give you more invisible presents every day."

"That's the most unusual gift I've ever had, Tony, and the nicest," his mother said as she set her card on the television set.

Discussion and Oral Exercises:

■ To stimulate a good discussion, you might begin with com-prehension questions such as these:

Where did Tony live? (In an apartment in the city)

Why wasn't his father at home? What kind of work did he do?

What kind of work do you think Tony's mother did? (She evidently worked part time in a restaurant. She could have been a cashier, cook, waitress, hostess, etc. The story does not specify, so that children can think about the kinds of work required in a restaurant.)

■ Do you think Tony's mother would rather have had a store-bought present?

■ Have you ever given anyone an invisible present? Do you like the idea? Could you give invisible presents at other times, besides on birthdays?

■ Think about some invisible presents you might give to your mother and your father. Could you give them to your brothers and sisters? To the other children in the class? To teachers?

75. Now What? (2-3)

Listening Experiences: Listening to problem situations in story form; thinking of solutions and making decisions.

Problem 1.

One Saturday afternoon Barbara's mother gave her some money and asked her to get a loaf of bread from a nearby grocery store. On the way she stopped to play on the monkey bars at the park playground. When she got to the store, the money was gone. She wondered what she should do. What do you think she did?

Discussion and Oral Exercises:

■ Some possible responses are given here, but they should be used only as pump primers, if pump primers are necessary. Encourage your children to think and discuss, and come to their own solutions.

Do you think Barbara was known to the owner of the store? If she was, what might she have done? (Asked for credit. Volunteered to help around the store to earn the money for the loaf of bread.)

Suppose Barbara didn't know the owner, or couldn't get credit or work, what else could she have done? Should she go home and explain what had happened? What might her mother say and do?

What would you have done in Barbara's place?

Problem 2.

Russel White sat stiffly in his seat. He was listening, but he wasn't taking part in the class discussion.

"The Indians were savages!" Arlene Eberhart was saying. "They killed the settlers for no reason at all!"

Russel's thoughts went back to his old home in Nevada. He and his mother and father had lived on the Paiute Indian Reservation in northwestern Nevada. They had made their living by fishing in Pyramid Lake. But the waters of Pyramid Lake were sinking lower and lower. The precious water was being diverted to the big cities in California, and now it was almost impossible to catch enough fish for their food or for sale to others. At last Russel's family had given up and moved to Los Angeles, where his father finally got a job on a road repair crew and his mother worked in a cleaning store.

The children at school didn't know he was an Indian. Some day, when he was big, he would go back again to his family's home, where it was so beautiful, and so peaceful and quiet under the blue sky.

Now Mrs. Preston was speaking. "We know now that the Indians have been treated very badly," she said. "Their land was taken from them, their water and food supplies were destroyed, and they were driven from their homes."

"But that happened after the Indians had murdered the white people!" Franklin Watts exclaimed. "I think they got what they deserved!"

Russel felt the blood rush to his face. He was proud to be an Indian. What did they know?

What do you think Russel did?

Discussion and Oral Exercises:

■ Do you think Russel joined in the discussion and defended the Indians? If he did, do you think he told the children that he was an Indian? If he did tell them, what do you think the children would have said?

Suppose he defended the Indians but didn't say he was an Indian. How might he feel? Suppose he decided not to say anything. How might he feel?

If you had been in Russel's place, what would you have done?

■ Where is Nevada? Where is Pyramid Lake, where Russel's people lived? (Use a map.) What is a reservation?

■ The Paiute Indians who live in the Pyramid Lake Reservations are called the Pyramid Lake Tribe. See if you can find stories about the Paiutes and other Indians of the Far West in the library. See what the encyclopedias can tell you about them.

76. Community Helpers (3)

Listening Experience: Listening to a story and becoming
aware of personal responsibility
toward the community one
lives in.

Mr. Arnold waited for the children to get settled after recess. When they were ready, he said, "Martin Luther has been
talking to me about an idea he has. I think you might like to
hear about it. All right, Martin Luther."

"Well," the boy began, "last Saturday my family went to
Isola Bella for a picnic. We hadn't been there for two or three
years and my sister and I were excited about going to the
aquarium and children's zoo after we ate."

Mr. Arnold broke in. "How many of you have been to Isola
Bella?" Eight or nine hands went up. He nodded. "Tell them
a little about Isola Bella, Martin Luther."

"Isola Bella is an island in the middle of the river, just
across from the downtown part of the city. It's been a park for
a long time. There's lots of trees and places to canoe, and you
can still fish in the river. There are places for picnics and
playgrounds. There's an aquarium and a plant place called
a . . . a . . ."

"Conservatory," Mr. Arnold volunteered.

"A conservatory, and a children's zoo. Big ships carrying
coal and ore and grain go down the river past Isola Bella."
Martin Luther paused. "My father said that when he was a
little kid, before the city got so built up, it was real pretty
there. He and his friends used to ride their bikes across the
bridge. Traffic wasn't so bad then. And they'd fish and play
baseball on the island."

A girl raised her hand. "Angela?" Mr. Arnold said.

"It's dirty over there. We don't go any more."

Several children started talking. Mr. Arnold said, "We'll
have discussion time after Martin Luther finishes talking. I
can tell many of you are interested."

Martin Luther said, "Angela is right. Isola Bella is a mess. There's junk all over—bottles and cans and paper—all kinds of stuff on the grass and along the beach and in the water. Even the big fountain is filled with junk. It was so bad at the picnic grounds that we ate our lunch in the car. Then we drove around the island and went home. We didn't even go to the children's zoo because it was so dirty everywhere."

"Go on," Mr. Arnold said.

"Well—my family tried to think what could be done. My parents say the city doesn't have enough money to keep the parks up because people litter so bad, and that if we want nice parks someone will need to clean them up and the people will have to stop littering."

"How? Who would do it?" several children asked.

"Our school isn't very far from Isola Bella. I wondered, if enough kids were interested, if we could go over there sometimes on Saturday and pick up some of that mess."

"My mother won't let me walk over there—it's too far," Angela said.

"Mine either," several children chorused.

"Maybe some of the parents would take carloads of kids," Martin Luther suggested. "My dad says he will."

The room buzzed as the children discussed ideas with their neighbors. After a time, Mr. Arnold said, "Does anyone have suggestions either for or against Martin Luther's idea?" He nodded to a boy, "Yes, Carlos?"

"There's hardly any good places to play here in the city. I didn't know about Isola Bella because we just moved here. I think my father might take a load of kids sometimes on Saturday."

"Good," Mr. Arnold said, "How many think Martin Luther's idea is worth a trial?" Every hand went up.

"William."

"My mother doesn't have a car. My sister and brother might help, too, if we could ride with someone."

"Fine. The more people we have the faster we can clean Isola Bella up."

A girl called. "I've thought of a poem!" The children laughed.

When they were quiet Mr. Arnold said, "Mary Ellen, is the poem about cleaning up Isola Bella?"

"Yeah."

"O.K. Tell us."

"Clean up!
Pick up!
It's all up to you!"

The children smiled and nodded their heads. Some said, "That's good," or "I like that!"

Carlos said, "Let's use it for our slogan!"

Shouts of "Yeah!" came from around the room. Someone said, "Put it on the board, Mary Ellen!"

Mary Ellen wrote her poem on the chalkboard in large letters, and everyone read it together.

Clean up!
Pick up!
It's all up to you!

They spent the rest of the afternoon planning. They decided that the big day would be a week from Saturday. They would make a list of all the parents who could promise to drive. Then anyone who needed a ride would be picked up at the school that Saturday morning at 10 o'clock, and would be returned there by 3:30 in the afternoon. Everyone would bring a sack lunch, and Mr. Arnold would furnish something to drink. Everyone would try to bring disposable plastic bags to put the litter into. Mr. Arnold would call the Parks and Recreation Department to find out where the filled bags should be left.

When the dismissal bell rang the room was still buzzing with plans for once more making Isola Bella a beautiful place.

Discussion and Oral Exercises:

■ The discussion can begin with questions based on the story, such as:

Was this school located in a small town or in a big city?
(Have children tell what clues they find in the story for
their answers.)

Do you think Martin Luther's plan could be successful?

Isola Bella is too big for one room to clean up all the
litter. How might the children interest other rooms in
the project?

■ The next set of questions leads the discussion into practical
problem-solving and decision-making.

Could we think of a project which would improve our
area? (School ground, the block surrounding the school,
local parks, rivers, beaches.)

How could we interest people outside of our school in
keeping our community beautiful? (By discussing it
with acquaintances, asking interested people to contribute time, getting other schools to do the same, etc.)

Do you think the local papers might publicize such a
project? How should we go about asking them?

■ Writing a class letter to all the local newspapers would be
an excellent Language Arts project